MACKEMS

VS

GEORDIES

Why Wearside is better than Tyneside

> **MACKEMS START HERE**

D1347758

First published 2008
by Black & White Publishing Ltd
29 Ocean Drive, Edinburgh EH6 6JL

1 3 5 7 9 10 8 6 4 2   08 09 10 11 12

ISBN: 978 1 84502 227 3

A CIP catalogue record for this book is available from the British Library.

Typeset by RefineCatch Limited, Bungay, Suffolk
Printed and bound by Norhaven A/S, Denmark

INTRODUCTION

Just to give you the flavour of how much Mackems and Geordies mutually detest each other, try this little jibe from the Newcastle terraces: Thieves broke into the trophy room of the Stadium of Shite, as the Geordies have lovingly christened Sunderland's Stadium of Light, and stole the entire contents. Police are looking for a fifty foot red and white stripy carpet.

In a survey of UK football fans, Newcastle fans have proved to be the most likely to have had sex in the shower. In the survey, carried out for a leading toiletries firm, 86% of Newcastle fans said that they have enjoyed sex in the shower.

The other 14% said they hadn't even been to prison yet.

Or how about: A Geordie is leaving the ground after yet another Keegan tactical disaster. A prostitute comes up to him and says: "Do you fancy a blow job, pet?" He stares at her in that dim, Geordie-like way, and asks: "Will it affect me Giro?"

And, of course, traditionally there is no request to tea in Newcastle, more of a statement, delivered without the question mark, as in: "You'll have had your tea." These days, instead of the offer of a drink it is: "You'll be driving."

One Mackem woman summed up her feelings succinctly: "I wouldn't want to move to a place where you have to put on matching clothing to pick up the milk from the doorstep."

People in Newcastle equate breeding with good form, whereas in Sunderland they accept it as good fun. There is a fairly prevalent paranoid myth among Geordies that all Mackems want to move to Newcastle and drive down property values, just out of badness.

The people of the two cities have traditionally always regarded each other with the greatest possible loathing, mistrust and contempt. They are both absolutely right. This book is the proof.

These are hard hits and sneaky bits from the Mackem side, sharp jibes and bludgeoning diatribes, but it's just friendly rivalry really. To use the double positive negative, a figure of speech used in both cities: "Aye, reet."

1

GENERIC INSULTS

There are three kinds of people in England.

First, there are the Geordies. They keep the Sabbath – and everything else they can lay their hands on. They pray on their knees . . . and their neighbours.

Second, there are the Cockneys, who never know what they want, but are willing to fight for it anyway, in between complaints in a very high-pitched nasal whine.

Lastly, there are the Mackems, who consider themselves self-made men, thus relieving God of a terrible responsibility.

A quote from an economist who wishes to remain unidentified in case he becomes unidentified remains: "Sunderland is still transfixed by its days of industrial and shipbuilding glory in the 19th and 20th centuries. Newcastle is doing quite well in the 18th."

2

ATTITUDES AND INSULTS

The standard disparagement of "Fur coat and no knickers" that is applied by the Mackem to the Geordie to illustrate the pretension to gentility so despised in Sunderland is turned on its head by this tale of two girls going for a night out. One is from Sunderland, one is from Newcastle.

Newcastle girl says, "Hang on a minute, I'll have to put on my knickers."

Sunderland girl looks shocked and says, "Knickers! On a night out?"

Another Sunderland phrase that sums this up:

Curtains at the window and no sheets on the bed.

What do Geordies use as a form of contraception?

A: Their personalities.

Q: What do you do if you see a Geordie with half a face?

A: Stop laughing and reload!

A Geordie, finally roused by a Mackem's needling, protested that he was born a Geordie and hoped to die a Geordie. "Christ Almighty," said the Mackem, "have you no ambition at all?"

Mackems travel to Newcastle, Geordies make expeditions to Sunderland. And they are not tense while in Sunderland – just terribly, terribly alert.

Said by a Sunderland man of a hypocritical Newcastle man when informed of his demise, "No doubt he'll get into heaven, but God won't like him. And it will be mutual."

You get more laughs at a Sunderland funeral than at a wedding in Newcastle.

In Newcastle, about the only concession to gaiety is a striped shroud.

A Mackem girl and a Geordie guy are in a bar when the girl notices something strange about the Wellington boots the guy's wearing.

She says to him, "Excuse me, but why does one of

your wellies have an L on it, and the other one's got an R on it?"

The Geordie smiles, puts down his pint of Boggles Trout Piss and replies, "Well, I am a little bit dense, you see. The one with the R is for my right foot and the one with the L is for my left foot."

"A'reet!" exclaims the Mackem. "So THAT'S why my knickers have got C&A on them."

A Mackem woman driver is pulled over by a policeman on the way out of Newcastle. "Is there a problem, officer?"

"Yes madam, you were speeding."

"Really?"

"May I see your licence please?"

"I'd give it to you but I don't have one."

"Don't have one?"

"No. Lost it after drunk driving four times."

"I see ... May I see your vehicle registration papers please?"

"No. Can't do that either."

"Why not?"

"Well . . . I stole this car."

"Stole it?"

"Yes, after I killed and chopped up the owner."

"You what?"

"Lost my temper. It was messy. His body is in a pile of plastic bags in the boot if you want to see."

The policeman looks at the woman for a second, then backs away to his car and calls for reinforcements. Within minutes there are more police cars circling them. A police sergeant approaches the car. He clears his throat, then calls to her, "Madam, please step out of and away from your vehicle."

She does so. "Is there a problem, sir?"

"One of my officers told me that you have stolen this car and murdered the owner."

"Murdered the owner?"

"Yes. Could you open the boot of your car please?"

She does, and they both look down into a dusty, empty space.

"Is this your car, madam?"

"Yes. Here are the registration papers."

The sergeant scans through them and sees that they are in order.

"My officer claims that you do not have a driving licence."

The woman rummages through her bag then hands her licence to the puzzled sergeant.

"Mrs Smith, my officer told me you didn't have a licence, that you stole this car, and that you murdered and dismembered the owner."

"I'll bet the lying Geordie bastard told you I was speeding too!"

A young Geordie stockbroker makes a ton of dough from a somewhat dodgy deal and celebrates not being caught by going out and buying a brand new Ferrari 550. He takes it out for a spin and, intoxicated by the speed and handling, is nearly in Sunderland before he looks out and notices where he is. Panicking slightly when he discovers that he has to get off the motorway in Mackemland to turn, he nevertheless does and is stopped at a red traffic light.

An old Mackem on a moped pulls up next to him. The old man looks over the sleek, shiny car and asks, "What kind of motor have you got there, son?"

The young man replies, "A Ferrari 550 – it cost 100 grand."

"That's a lot of cash," says the old man. "Why did it cost so much?"

"Because this car can do up to 220 miles an hour!" he says proudly.

The moped driver asks, "Mind if I take a look inside?"

"No problem, just try not to breathe on the

upholstery," replies the owner. So the old man pokes his head in the window and looks around.

Then sitting back on his moped, the old man says, "That's a pretty nice car you've got there, but I think I'll stick with my moped. I've seen the day, though, when I would have given you a race."

Just then, the light changes to green so the guy decides to show the old man just what his car can do. He shouts: "Right, you Mackem coffin-dodger," floors it, and within 15 seconds the speedometer reads 160 mph.

Suddenly, he notices a dot in his rear view mirror. It seems to be getting closer. He slows down to see what it could be and suddenly, *whooooooossssshhhh*! Something whips past him, going much faster.

"What could be going faster than my flying machine?" the young man asks himself. He floors the accelerator again and takes the Ferrari up to 200 mph. Then, up ahead of him, he sees that it is the old man on the moped.

Amazed that the moped could pass his Ferrari and just a little bit apprehensive about the insult, he gives it some more welly and passes the moped at 210 mph. *Whhhhooooooossssssshhhh*!!! He's feeling pretty good until he looks in his mirror and sees the old man gaining on him again.

Astounded by the speed of this old guy he floors

the accelerator and takes the Ferrari all the way up to 220 mph. Not ten seconds later, he sees the moped bearing down on him again. The Ferrari is flat out and there's nothing he can do. He is shitting bricks by now, as he thinks that the Mackem is out for revenge.

Suddenly, the moped ploughs into the back of his Ferrari, demolishing the rear end. He skids to a halt as the car catches fire. The young man jumps out, wishing he'd insured it, and unbelievably, the old man is still alive. He runs up to the mangled old guy and says, "Oh my God! Is there anything I can do for you?"

The old man says . . .

"Before I burn to death, please unhook my fucking braces from your wing mirror!"

Sunderland's kids are not better natural fighters than Newcastle kids. It is just that they are better trained and have better weaponry.

How many Geordie graduates does it take to screw in a light bulb?

One: he stands still and the world revolves around him.

Tom the Mackem is up in court in Sunderland, running down two Geordies with his car. The ju says: "Now we have heard the evidence given, h⟨ ⟩ you anything to say before I pass sentence?"

"Well," Tom says, "I had been out for a drive and I was making my way home, doing 30 mph, minding the speed limit, when out from between two cars stepped these two people, and I hit them. One came through the windscreen, the other went over the hedge."

The judge looks at Tom and says: "We have all heard the eyewitness reports, would you like to try again and tell the court what happened?"

"Ok," says Tom. "Well, I was trying to get home for my tea, the traffic had been bad, got to an open bit of road, I might have been doing about 45 mph in the 30 zone, when these two poofy-looking guys stepped out in front of me and I hit them. One came through the windscreen the other went over the hedge."

"Getting a bit more like the evidence now," says the judge. "Would you like one more chance?"

"Oh God. Ok," says Tom. "Right, I'd been at the Sunderland/Newcastle game and the bastards beat us three-nil. I was pissed off so I was belting along at 75 mph to get to the pub to drown my sorrows, when I see these two Newcastle fans walking along the road in their poncy fifty quid shirts. So I think, right you bastards, mounted the pavement, chased them for a bit, then got the twats. One came through the windscreen and the other went over the hedge."

"That's better," said the judge. "It's now my duty to pass sentence. We'll charge one with breaking and entering, and the other for leaving the scene of the crime."

Little Mackem Tommy was sitting on a park bench on a day out in Newcastle munching on one Mars Bar after another. After the sixth a Geordie on the bench across from him said, "Son, you know eating all that fat and chocolate isn't good for you. It will give you acne, rot your teeth, and make you fat."

Little Mackem Tommy replied, "My grandfather lived to be 107 years old."

The man asked, "Did your grandfather eat six Mars Bars at a time?"

Little Mackem Tommy answered, "No, he minded his own fucking business!"

3

SIGNS YOU'VE BEEN IN NEWCASTLE TOO LONG

You think Mackems are unsavoury, but you've never met any as you are too scared to go to Sunderland after dark in case somebody steals one of your eleven mobile phones.

You think it is your God-given right to slag all the other English cities.

You think paying £10 for a 3 minute cab ride is perfectly acceptable.

You will sulk at the champagne being warm at Christmas.

You sulk if there are no after-club parties because you can't possibly go to bed before 11.30 am the next day.

You will sulk if you don't manage to spend £1000 on your credit card in your lunch hour.

In Newcastle a dog can teach a boy many things – fidelity, perseverance, and to turn around three times before lying down.

In Newcastle they say: "If at first you don't succeed, redefine success."

In Sunderland they say: "If at first you don't succeed, ah, fuck it."

In Newcastle everyone can do one thing better than everybody else. It's usually reading their own handwriting on the confession.

A Mackem stood watching a Geordie fishing. He noticed that the man dipped his bait into a bottle by his side before each cast and was astounded to find that he had a dozen fine trout flapping on the bank beside him within five minutes. He became curious and went down to ask what his secret was.

"No secret, but just a bottle of 50-year-old malt whisky. The fish just can't get enough of it."

So the man rushed back to his place and got out his own fishing rod. Oddly enough, he didn't have any 50-year-old malt whisky to hand so he decided to try out some of his freshly-bought bottle of Buckfast instead.

The next day the Geordie was walking alongside the river and met the man coming the other way with a salmon the size of a small elephant slung over his shoulder. He prudently restrained his natural curiosity regarding the existence of a fishing permit and said: "Congratulations. I'm glad to see the single malt whisky trick worked for you too."

The Mackem grinned back and said: "You should try the electric soup instead. When I got this fish out of the water it took me five minutes to get the worm to let go of his throat."

After pulling a Mackem over for speeding, the member of Newcastle's finest started to lecture him about his speed, pompously implying that the Mackem didn't know any better and trying to make him feel as uncomfortable as possible. He finally started writing out the ticket, but had to keep swatting at some flies buzzing around his head. The Mackem asked, "Having some problems with circle flies there, are you?"

The policeman paused to take another swipe and said, "Well, yes, if that's what they are. I've never heard of circle flies."

The Mackem was pleased to enlighten the cop. "Circle flies are most common on farms. They're called circle flies because you almost always find them circling the backside of a horse."

The policeman continues writing for a moment then says, "Are you trying to call me a horse's arse?"

"Oh no, officer," the Mackem replies. "I have too much respect for your particular force and police officers for that."

"Good job," the cop says snidely, then goes back to writing him up.

After a long pause the Mackem adds, "Hard to fool those flies, though."

What's the difference between a Geordie man and a large pizza?

A large pizza can feed a family of four.

A Geordie, an Irishman, a Mackem and a Tory MP were sharing a railway carriage.

The MP was reading the *Daily Mail*, and after a time he sighed with exasperation, screwed his paper up into a ball and threw it into the wastebasket. The other passengers were shocked and asked why he had done that. He said: "Well, in this country, opinions like those are ten a penny."

The Geordie was drinking a whisky he had brought from the bar when a similar mood of exasperation seemed to descend on him and he threw the glass in the bin. "Why did you do that?" asked the others. "Well, in my salary bracket," said the Geordie, "whiskies like that are ten a penny."

The journey continued and the Irishman began to get restless and flung his book to join the other discards. "Before you ask," he said, "in my part of the world authors are ten a penny."

The Mackem had been sitting quietly when he suddenly lunged forward, pinioned the Geordie and stuffed him headfirst into the bin. "Why did you do that?" they asked him.

He said: "Felt like it."

This Geordie walks into a bookshop. He asks the clerk, "Can I have a play by Shakespeare?"

The assistant says: "Of course, sir. Which one?"

The Geordie says, "William."

What they drink in Newcastle a lot is advocaat, which sounds, looks and tastes like it has been distilled from the juice of the backbones of lawyers.

The phone rang in a Newcastle pub and the landlord answered it.

"This is the IRA," the voice said. "There's a bomb in your pub and you've got five minutes to get out."

The owner put the phone down and went back to the bar.

"Last orders, everyone!" he shouted.

A bus carrying only ugly Geordies and the only ugly Mackem crashes into an oncoming truck, and everyone inside dies. They then get to meet their maker and, because of the grief they have experienced, he decides to grant them one wish each before they enter Paradise.

They're all lined up, and God asks the first one what the wish is.

"I want to be gorgeous," he says, so God snaps his fingers and it is done. The second one in line hears this and says: "I want to be gorgeous too."

Another snap of is fingers and the wish is granted. This goes on for a while, but when God is halfway down the line, the Mackem, who is the last in line, starts laughing. When there are only ten people left, this guy is rolling on the floor, laughing his bollocks off.

Finally, God reaches the guy and asks him what his wish will be. The Mackem calms down and says: "Make them all ugly again."

A Mackem was made ashamed of his accent when working in Newcastle so he went south to get elocution lessons. He returned three years later, speaking perfect Queen's English and went out to celebrate with a drink, walking into the first establishment he could find.

"I say, my good man," his silky tones rang out. "Perhaps you could find me a bottle of chilled Bolly and one of your finest Havana cigars."

"You're from Sunderland, aren't you," said the proprietor.

"Good Lord, how ever did you possibly know," said the stunned and aggrieved Mackem.

"Well, you see," said the proprietor, "this is a butcher's."

The *Evening Chronicle* sent a reporter to interview the oldest man in Newcastle, Michael Snoddie.

"And exactly how old are you, Mr Snoddie?" asked the young reporter.

"One hundred and three years old today, son," croaked Snoddie.

"And I'm sure you've seen a fair few changes in your time, sir."

"I have indeed, son. And I've been against them all."

A young Mackem couple went to visit an estate agent in Newcastle.

"Right," said the agent. "Just tell me your starting price, then we'll all have a good laugh and take it from there."

Posh Newcastle question: What do you do when you see an endangered animal that is eating an endangered plant?

Answer: Make sure that you don't make eye contact with anyone.

In Newcastle, if a mute swears, his mother washes his hands with soap. In Sunderland they just give him the finger.

Newcastle folk are so narrow-minded that even when they get an idea it comes out neatly folded.

Newcastle, where no shirt is too young to be stuffed.

4

YOU KNOW THAT YOU ARE WORKING FOR THE GOVERNMENT IN NEWCASTLE:

When someone asks about what you do for a living, you lie.

You get really excited about a 2% pay raise.

Your biggest loss from a system crash is that you lose your best jokes.

Your supervisor doesn't have the ability to do your job.

You sit in a cubicle smaller than your bedroom cupboard.

Computer specialists know less about computers than your teenager.

Lunch is like another scheduled meeting, but shorter.

If you see a good-looking person you know they are a visitor.

Management thinks a business trip with uncompensated mandatory weekend travel is a perk.

Although you have a telephone, pager, email, fax,

company distribution, mail and co-workers sitting right on the other side of the partition . . . communication is a continuing problem.

You know, and everyone who works with you knows, that your performance is superior, but 'satisfactory' is the highest level on the documented performance rating.

You work 200 hours for the £100 bonus and jubilantly say 'Oh great, thanks very much!'

When workers screw up they are transferred to another office to be someone else's problem; when management screws up they are promoted.

Your boss's favourite lines are 'when you get a few minutes,' 'in your spare time,' 'when you're free' and 'I have an opportunity for you'.

Training is something spoken about but never seen.

A holiday is something you'll get next year . . . maybe.

The worst possible reputation comes from being the initiator of a complaint.

The war between Sunderland and Newcastle will not determine who is right – only who is left. And it won't start with N.

As they say in Sunderland: "Dear God, grant me patience, but get a move on, man!"

Trying to find an honest man in Newcastle is like trying to find a fart in a Jacuzzi.

A Mackem walks into a bar and says, "Give me a triple vodka!" He quickly downs it and says, "Another!" Again he sinks it and demands "Another!"

He keeps on drinking until, after his eighth, the barman says, "How man, you drink like you've got a problem. Do you want to talk about it?"

The guy says, "Ten years I've been with my wife, even though she's a Geordie. I left work early today, to surprise her. I came home to find her in bed with my best friend."

"What did you say to them?" asks the barman.

"I told her to get back to Newcastle, and I told him 'Bad dog, bad dog!'"

The Mackem was through in Newcastle for the night and was having a quiet pint. A live band filed in to the pub and started to play a selection of Magpie songs. As tune followed tune, all in praise of the men from mighty United, he leaned over the bar and shouted in the barman's ear: "Is it just all Geordie songs or does this band play anything on request?" he asked.

"Oh yes, they do," said the barman.

"That's great," said the Mackem. "Ask them to go outside and play hopscotch."

Newcastle United: A t-shirt and merchandising team, also plays football, but not nearly as well.

One of the Mackem pastimes is to visit Newcastle to play a game called Spot the Mackem. If you spot one you win and can go home immediately. Nobody has ever won.

The two Geordie school inspectors were in an estate in Sunderland waiting for a taxi, having been silly enough to leave their car outside the school. They noticed a Fort Knox of a pub and took note of the rough hand-lettered sign on the door, which read: "We have plain drinks and we have fancy drinks."

Reading this, the two Geordies smirked at each other and went in, scuffing their feet through the sawdust on the floor. "Last night's furniture," said one, grinning condescendingly.

There was a barman with his back to them washing glasses, so they started talking. One of them, addressing space, said: "Seeing that they serve fancy drinks here, I'll have a gin rickey, maybe with a smoked olive. What are you going to have?" he added, addressing his fellow would-be joker.

"Good choice," said the other. "I think I'll try a dry martini cocktail, made with French vermouth, and a spiced cocktail onion, one of the coloured ones. Pink, perhaps."

Without shifting his position or lifting his eyes from his work the barman said: "I can kick the arse of any given two Geordie space-wasters in 11.2 seconds. That's my record, but I know I can beat it with you two. And I haven't even turned round yet."

5

THE NEWCASTLE CHRISTMAS CAROL

Late last week, I was rushing around trying to get some last minute shopping done. I was stressed out and not thinking very fondly of the Festive season right then. It was dark, cold, and wet as I was loading my car with gifts that I felt obliged to buy. I noticed that I was missing a receipt that I might need later. So, mumbling under my breath, I retraced my steps to the shop entrance.

As I was searching the wet pavement for the lost receipt, I heard a quiet sobbing. The crying was coming from a poorly dressed boy of about 12 years old. He was short and thin. He had no coat and was just wearing a ragged flannel shirt to protect him from the cold night's chill.

Oddly enough, he was holding a hundred pound note in his hand. Thinking that he had become sep-arated from his parents in the busy shop, I asked him what was wrong. He told me his sad story. He said that he came from a large family. He had three brothers and four sisters. His father had died when he was nine years old. His mother was poorly educated and worked at two full time jobs. She made very little to support her large family.

Nevertheless, she had managed to skimp and save two hundred pounds to buy her children Christmas presents. The young boy had been dropped off, by his mother, on the way to her second job. He was to use the money to buy presents for all his siblings and save just enough to take the bus home. He had not even entered the shop when an older boy grabbed one of the hundred pound notes and disappeared into the night.

"Why didn't you scream for help?" I asked.

The boy said, "I did."

"And nobody came to help you?" I wondered.

The boy stared at the pavement and sadly shook his head.

"How loud did you scream?" I inquired.

The soft-spoken boy looked up and meekly whispered, "Help me!"

I realised that absolutely no one could have heard that boy cry for help.

So I grabbed his other hundred and ran to the car.

What's the difference between Geordies and a jet engine?

A jet engine eventually stops whining.

A Mackem designer, who has designs on moving to Newcastle and wishes to remain anonymous (easy, peasy lemon squeezy in Newcastle, one would think) claims that Newcastle women wear: "Clothing that looks as if it was designed and made by people who had had clothes described to them, but who had never seen any."

Two Geordie ladies had been enticed to Sunderland for the sales and were resting their barking dogs in a tearoom, having spent two hours looking for the cheapest one. One said to the friendly waitress who asked what they wanted: "None of your Sunderland banter, thanks, just tea, and I hope my cup is clean."

The waitress bustled off and returned with a pot of tea a moment or so later, saying cheerily: "Which one of you wanted the clean cup?"

Man walking along a road in the countryside comes across a shepherd and a huge flock of sheep. He tells the shepherd, "I will bet you £100 against one of your sheep that I can tell you the exact number in this flock." The shepherd thinks it over; it's a big flock, so he takes the bet. "973," says the man. The shepherd is astonished, because that is exactly right. He says, "OK, I'm a man of my word, take an animal." The man picks one up and begins to walk away.

"Wait," cries the shepherd. "Let me have a chance to get even. Double or nothing that I can guess your exact occupation." The man says okay. "You are an economist for the Home Office in Newcastle," says the shepherd. "Amazing!" responds the man. "You are exactly right! But tell me, how did you deduce that?"

"Well," says the shepherd, "put down my dog and I'll tell you."

Newcastle estate dwellers love cats. They taste just like chicken.

"You seem to have more than the average share of intelligence for a man of your background," said the Geordie advocate to a Mackem witness.

"If I wasn't under oath, I'd return the compliment," replied the witness.

Two Geordies boarded a flight. One sat in the window seat, the other sat in the middle seat. Just before takeoff, a Mackem got on and took the aisle seat next to the two Geordies. The Mackem kicked off his shoes, wiggled his toes and was settling in when the guy in the window seat said: "I think I'll get up and get a beer."

"No problem," said the Mackem. "I'll get it for you." While he was gone, one of the Geordies picked up the Mackem's shoe and spat in it.

When he returned with the beer, the other guy said, "That looks good, I think I'll have one too."

Again, the Mackem obligingly went to fetch it and while he was gone, the other guy picked up the other shoe and spat in it. The Mackem returned and they all sat back and enjoyed the flight. As the plane was landing, the Mackem slipped his feet into his shoes and knew immediately what had happened.

He turned to them and asked passionately, "How long must this go on? This fighting between our cities? This hatred? This animosity? This spitting in shoes and pissing in beers?"

Q: What do you say to a Geordie with money?

A: Anything you like, he's not listening . . . and, if he inherited it, he can't even see you.

"What's this diet you're doing?" asked the Geordie of the Mackem.

"It's called the booze diet, I've lost three days already."

Sunderland recipe. Take a pound. Buy chips. Put salt and vinegar on them. Eat them.

Newcastle recipe. Take a pound. Buy chips. Pretend you made them. Eat them.

Sunderland saying: As cheap as chips.

Newcastle saying: As dear as chips.

Two prisoners are talking about their crimes:
    George: "I robbed a bank, and they gave me 20 years."
    Jim: "Hmm. I killed a man, and I'm here for 3 days."
    George: "What? I rob a bank and get 20 years; you kill a man and get 3 days?"
    Jim: "Well, it was a Newcastle lawyer."

Geordies are even allowed to travel the world and this year one was reported as being the only survivor of a plane crash when a jumbo went down in the South China Sea. The man was found clinging to a piece of board the size of a fag packet but had not been touched by the sharks which had quickly snapped up his fellow passengers. The Mate of the rescue ship was a Mackem and when the Australian skipper of the rescue vessel expressed astonishment at the survival of the Geordie he pointed to the dripping exhausted man lying flat on his back on the deck and said: "See that t-shirt? It says 'Newcastle for the Premier league title'. Not even a shark is going to swallow that."

Newcastle District Council: so many fiddles going on that they hired Yo Yo Ma to conduct them.

Geordies comb their hair in order to make an impression on the pillow.

Newcastle ladies say things like: "Oh Janet, he was just a bit too friendly . . . a real Mackem. He came up to me on the bus and put his hand up my skirt . . . you know the Jaeger one with the pleats."

There is a fairly prevalent paranoid myth among Geordies that all Mackems want to move to

Newcastle and drive down property values, just out of badness. One Mackem woman summed up her feeling succinctly: "I wouldn't want to move to a place where you have to put on matching clothing to pick up the milk from the doorstep."

Sunderland has been described as savagely egalitarian, Newcastle as civilised fascism.

A Mackem family are on a trip to rellies in Newcastle. On the way back into town on the bus they find themselves behind a fur-coated lady, whose eyes rake them disapprovingly as she sits down with an almost audible sniff. The youngest child has one of those enormous drippy lollipops and is eventually wiping the drips off on the lady's collar. The Mackem mum notes the lady's discomfort, just as she had noted the disapproval earlier, and says; "Jasmine, stop that!," then waits till she sees the lady relax a fraction before continuing: "You'll get your lolly all hairy."

The Magpie scouts have been scouring the country, offering their usual sweets and buttons for players and wages, but it is Knockback City all over the place. They finally find a youngster who looks very tasty and they get him along to St James for a trial, where he puts on an astonishing display. He then confesses that the surroundings have made him play better as he is a lifelong Newcastle fan, and says that he will play for no wages.

He is hustled into the office for a quick physical, but the doc eventually, as everything else is looking good, goes: "Oh-oh."

"What's the matter?" asks the lad.

"You're Jewish, aren't you?" says the doc.

"Yes," he replies.

"Sorry, son, you'll not get a game here."

"Why not?" says the affronted boy, sensing perse-cution.

"Jesus, son," sighs the doc, "everybody knows that you have to be a complete dick to play for United."

6

STUPID GEORDIES

The Mackem and the Geordie were on a parachute training course. The Geordie jumped first, pulled the rip-cord and started to float down. The Mackem followed, but when he pulled his cord, nothing happened. When he pulled the emergency cord, again nothing happened. As the Mackem plummeted past, the Geordie shouted, "So we're in a race are we?" and ripped off his parachute.

7

MACKEM PHILOSOPHY

There are two golden rules for life in Sunderland:
1) Never tell people everything.

An Evertonian sharing a train up from London with a Sunderland pal on their way to play Newcastle United and Man Utd was heard to comment: "No matter if we win or lose our games, we will still be winners in the game of life, because when they waken up tomorrow they'll still be from Newcastle and Manchester."

Casual Sunderland acceptance of immigrants:
"Wonder what their chips will be like."

In Newcastle there is a comfortable time-lag of a century or so intervening between the perception that something ought to be done and a serious attempt to do it.

In Newcastle real friends help you move. In Sunderland real friends help you move bodies.

Geordie: "Hard work pays off in the future."
  Mackem: "Laziness pays off now."

Sunderland saying: The Newcastle gene pool would be none the worse of a little chlorine.

Sunderland saying: He who laughs last thinks slowest.

In Newcastle, a penny saved is a penny earned. In Sunderland, a penny saved is just stupid. What can you buy with a penny?

Mackem to Geordie: I've seen better looking faces on pirate flags.

Sunderland saying: Ambition is a poor excuse for not having enough sense to be lazy.

In Newcastle they say: "Don't force it, be careful." In Sunderland they say: "Get a bigger hammer."

Newcastle! Too many freaks, not enough circuses.

Newcastle's suburbia: where they tear up the trees and then name streets after them.

Mackem threat to Geordie: You! Off my planet!

Nothing is ever a complete failure – it can always serve as a bad example. Look at Newcastle.

As they say in Newcastle, drugs may be the road to nowhere, but at least they're the scenic route.

Newcastle City Council rule: If two wrongs don't make a right, try three.

Sunderland saying: Before you criticise someone, you should walk a mile in their shoes. That way you are a mile away from them and you have their shoes.

Sunderland saying: If you lend someone £20 and never see that person again, it was probably worth it. So stab his brother.

Sunderland saying: Dance like no one's watching.
Newcastle saying: Don't dance. Everybody's watching.

Observation by a psychologist (a Geordie): In Sunderland people put the lights on first, then draw the blinds. In Newcastle they draw the blinds first, make sure that no one can see in, and then put the lights on.

8

JUST DESERTS

A Mackem and a Geordie get into a car accident, and it's a bad one. Both cars are totally demolished, but amazingly, neither of them is hurt.

After they crawl out of their cars, the Geordie says, "So you're a Mackem, that's interesting. I'm a Geordie. Wow! Just look at our cars. They're totally wrecked, but fortunately we're unhurt. This must be a sign from God that we should meet and be friends, putting our differences behind us."

The Mackem replies, "I agree with you completely, this must indeed be a sign from God!" He continues, "And look at this – here's another miracle. My car is completely demolished but this bottle of whisky didn't break. Surely God wants us to drink this and celebrate our good fortune."

Then he hands the bottle to the Geordie. He nods his head in agreement, opens it and takes a few big swigs from the bottle, then hands it back to the Mackem. He takes the bottle, immediately puts the cap back on, and hands it back to the Geordie.

He asks: "Aren't you having any?"

The Mackem grins and then replies, "No. I think I'll just wait for the cops."

9

MACKEMS AND DRINK

Newcastle (and Sunderland) breakfast: A bottle of Buckfast, a big lump of stotty cake and a spaniel. The spaniel is for eating the stotty cake.

Sunderland saying: There is no such thing as a large vodka.

The Mackem doctor checked over his patient and said with a puzzled frown: "I can't really tell what the trouble is. I think it must be due to drink."

Mackem patient, understandingly: "Oh, that's all right doctor. I'll come back when you're sober."

In Sunderland a seven course meal is a bottle of cider and six cans of beer.

Sunderland saying: You aren't drunk if you can lie on the floor without holding on.

Sunderland proverb: "Never drink whisky without water and never drink water without whisky."

Jimmy the inebriate Mackem was always coming home from the pub in the early hours of the morning. Eventually he found this note from his wife – "The day before yesterday you came home yesterday morning. Yesterday you came home this morning. So if today you come home tomorrow morning you will find that I left you yesterday."

Having returned at 3am from the office party, very much the worse for wear, Jimmy the inebriate Mackem woke his wife with a dreadful noise. She came downstairs to find him kicking the fridge and shouting: "The cash machine isn't workin'."

A man called at Jimmy the inebriate Mackem's door collecting for the Home for Chronic Alcoholics. His wife answered the door and said, "Call back after closing time. You can collect my husband then."

Jimmy the inebriate Mackem arrived at Sadie's flat with a dozen cans of beer and a bottle of rum. After half an hour of chat, Jimmy eventually asked: "When are the others coming for the party?" Sadie looked surprised. "The party was last night. And you were here!"

A Geordie entered a bar and accidentally stood beside a Mackem, who immediately initiated a conversation. After they had chatted for a while the Mackem asked: "Where are you from?" The Geordie replied, "I'm from the finest city in the world." The Mackem lowered his brows and said with that indefinable aura of menace: "Aye? That's not a Mackem accent." The pub was open again in a few days.

"Alcohol is your trouble," said the judge to Jimmy the inebriate Mackem. "Alcohol alone is responsible for your present predicament." Jimmy the inebriate Mackem looked pleased as he said, "Thank you, judge. Everyone else says it's my fault!"

Alex the Mackem told his friends that he couldn't come to the pub because his wife was doing bird imitations – she was watching him like a hawk.

Paddy the Mackem decided to call his father-in-law "The Exorcist" because every time he came to visit he made the spirits disappear.

George the Mackem's long-suffering Geordie wife was fed up with her husband's unfortunate fondness of a not-so-small drink. Most evenings he would roll home from the pub considerably the worse for wear. His wife resolved to cure him. On Halloween, she put a bedsheet over her head, hid behind the hydrangea at the front door, and waited for her wayward man to come home. Eventually he staggered up the path.

His wife, in disguise, jumped out from behind the bushes, and cried out, "George! I'm the Devil! And I've come to warn you ..."

"The Devil, are you?" George interrupted. "Then you must come in and have a drink with me. I do believe I'm married to your sister."

"Moderation, sir. Moderation is my rule. Nine or ten is reasonable refreshment, but after that it is likely to degenerate into drinking."

Anonymous, but definitely not a Geordie.

10

HEAVEN

A Geordie dies and goes to heaven. He knocks on the pearly gates and out walks St. Peter.

"Hello, mate," says St. Peter, "I'm sorry, no Geordies in heaven."

"What?" exclaims the man, astonished.

"You heard – no Geordies."

"But, but, but, I've been a good man," replies the Geordie.

"Oh really," says St. Peter. "What have you done, then?"

"Well," said the guy, "three weeks before I died, I gave £10 to the starving children in Africa."

"Oh," says St. Peter. "Anything else?"

"Well, two weeks before I died I also gave £10 to the homeless."

"Hmmm. Anything else?"

"Yeah. A week before I died I gave £10 to the Albanian orphans."

"Okay," said St. Peter, "You wait here a minute while I have a word with the Big Man."

Ten minutes pass before St. Peter returns. He looks the bloke in the eye and says, "I've had a word with God and he agrees with me. Here's your thirty quid back. Now fuck off."

A quiet looking young man knocks on the pearly gates and asks to be let in. St. Peter says, "I don't know. Have you ever done anything good, like given money to the poor?"

"No," replied the man.

"Helped a widow or orphan?"

"No," replied the man.

"Helped a little old lady across a street?"

"No."

"Well then, why should I let you in?"

"I did do something very brave once," he said.

"And what was that?" asked Peter.

"I went to Sunderland on the train and ran around Sunderland station shouting: 'Mackems are all scumbags.'"

"My, that is brave! When did you do that?"

"About 3 minutes ago."

St. Peter was manning the Pearly Gates when forty Mackems showed up. Never having seen any gadgies from Sunderland at Heaven's door, St. Peter said he would have to check with God. After hearing the news, God instructed him to admit the ten most virtuous from the group. A few minutes later, St. Peter returned to God breathless and said, "They're gone."

"What? All of the Mackems are gone?" asked God.

"Yes," replied St. Peter. "And the Pearly Gates!"

11

HELL

One of the only two plumbers in Sunderland to charge reasonable fees died and was sent to Hell by mistake. Eventually it was realised in Heaven that there was an honest Mackem plumber in the wrong place so St. Peter telephoned (on the hot line, naturally) to Satan.

"Have you got an honest plumber there?"

"Yes."

"He's ours, so can you send him up?"

"You can't have him!"

"Why not?"

"Because he's the only one who understands air conditioning. It's really cool down here now."

"Send him up at once," shouted St. Peter, "or we'll sue."

"You'll sue?" laughed the voice at the other end. "And where will you get hold of a lawyer in Heaven? They're all either here or in Newcastle."

The preferred Mackem way of dying: "I want to die

peacefully in my sleep, like my grandfather. Not kicking and screaming like the passengers on his bus."

Sunderland saying: No man is an island, except in his bath.

Here's attitude: Two Mackems were captured by the Romans and were thrown into a cell at the arena prior to being thrown to the lions. An instant friendship developed, as it does between Mackems, and they were chatting away amicably as they were led out in chains to the lions' den. They were thrown in and one was asking the other: "So when is Jean's baby due?" to receive the reply: "I'll tell you later. The lions are coming."

And there is another lions' den tale of a posse of Blakelaw kids on a bus trip to a safari park managing to escape from the bus and their guardians and prowl around outside among the animals. A keeper, concerned for their safety came running over, shouting: "The lions, boys, the lions!" to receive the reply: "We nivva touched your lions."

It is a miracle that curiosity survives any formal education, especially the Newcastle public school model, which may well have given rise to the saying: "Sunderland people want to know, Newcastle people think they know already."

Yesterday a friend was travelling to Sunderland on a flight from Paris. A man of Arabic appearance got off the plane and my friend noticed he had left his bag behind. She grabbed the bag and ran after him, caught up with him in the terminal and handed it to him.

He was extremely grateful and reached into the bag, which appeared to contain large bundles of money. He looked around to make sure nobody was looking and whispered.

"I can never repay your kindness, but I will try with words of advice for you: Stay away from Newcastle!"

My friend was genuinely terrified. "Is there going to be an attack?" she asked him.

"No," he whispered back. "It's a shithole."

12

MEAN GEORDIES

A Mackem, a Cockney and a Geordie were in a bar and had just started on a new round of drinks when a fly landed in each glass of beer. The Mackem took his out on the blade of his knife. The Cockney picked his out and put it in his pocket for later. The Geordie lifted his one up carefully by the wings and held it above his glass, saying: "Go on, spit it out."

George the crafty Geordie had become a bit hard of hearing, but he didn't want to pay for a hearing aid. So he bought a piece of flex, put one end in his top pocket and the other end in his ear. It didn't help his hearing but he found that people spoke to him more loudly.

A Geordie matron, who was rather stingy, was giving a drink to a tradesman who had done a good job. As she handed him his glass she said it was extra good whisky, being fourteen years old. "Well, pet," said the man, regarding his glass sorrowfully, "It's very small for its age."

George the careful Geordie took his girlfriend out for the evening. They returned to her flat just before midnight and, as she kissed him goodnight, she said: "Be careful on your way home. I'd hate anyone to rob you of all the money you've saved this evening."

There was understandable scepticism when it was suggested that Napoleon Bonaparte was the grandson of a Geordie from Cowgate. But now it has been pointed out that there is further proof that Napoleon was indeed from there – apart from being a little loser, his hand was always under his jacket, to make sure no-one had lifted his wallet.

A visitor to a Newcastle bar was surprised to find the beer only two pence a pint. The barman explained that it was the price to mark the centenary of the pub opening. The visitor noticed, however, that the bar was empty. "Are the regular customers not enjoying the special prices?" he asked. To which the barman replied: "They're waiting for the Happy Hour."

How do you persuade a Geordie to go on the roof? Tell him the drinks are on the house...

When a bus company was prevailed upon to increase the concessionary fare to frequent travellers so that they got six journeys instead of four for a pound, one elderly gentleman, renowned for his frugality, even in a community where frugal folk are common, was still unhappy.

"It's all foolishness," he declared. "Now we've got to walk to town six times instead of four times to save a pound!"

Did you hear about the Geordie who got caught making nuisance telephone calls? He kept reversing the charges.

A Sunderland prayer: "Oh Lord, we do not ask you to give us wealth. Just show us where it is."

A Newcastle prayer: "Oh Lord, we do not ask you to give us wealth. Just show us where the Mackems are."

Newcastle bureaucrats: A difficulty for every solution.

Pat called in to see his Geordie friend David to find he was stripping the wallpaper from the walls. Rather obviously, he remarked, "You're decorating, I see." To which David replied, "No, I'm moving house." If he had been a Mackem he would have been kidding.

Have you heard the rumour that the Grand Canyon was started by a Geordie who dropped a penny in a ditch?

Or the one about the Geordie who went out into the street the night before Christmas, blew up and burst a paper bag, and then told his kids that Santa had committed suicide.

Or the one about the Geordie who whispered to one of the Siamese twins, "Get rid of your sister, and I'll stand you a drink."

Or the one about the Geordie who wrote to an editor, "If you don't stop printing derogatory jokes about mean-spirited Geordies, I'll stop borrowing your damn magazine."

After discovering that they had won £15 million on the Lottery, Mr and Mrs Geordie sat down to discuss their future. Mrs Geordie announced: "After twenty years of washing other people's stairs, I can throw my old scrubbing brush away at last." Her husband agreed. "Of course you can, pet. We can easily afford to buy you a new one now."

Geordies have an infallible cure for sea-sickness. They lean over the side of the ship with a ten pence coin in their teeth.

In some Newcastle restaurants they heat the knives so you can't use too much butter. In Sunderland restaurants the knives are chained to the tables. With very short chains.

13

ATTITUDES AND INSULTS

English by birth; British by law; Mackem by the grace of God.

What are the two worst things about a Geordie?
    His (or her) face.

It was a party. The Mackem brought the Buckfast. The Irishman brought a crate of Guinness. The Scotsman brought a haggis. The Geordie brought his brother.

Suggestion for a t-shirt:
    Winning isn't everything
    Beating Newcastle is.

A Geordie has all the qualities of a poker, except its occasional warmth.

What's the difference between a tightrope and a Geordie?

A tightrope sometimes gives a little.

Geordie lifestyle tip: Increase the life of your carpets by rolling them up and keeping them in the loft.

"Is old Mick a typical Geordie?"

"Is he? He's saved all his toys for his second childhood."

The man who invented slow motion movies got the idea while watching a Geordie reaching for the bill in a restaurant.

How do you know when a Geordie is about to say something intelligent?

When he starts his sentence with, "A Mackem once told me..."

Geordie savings tip:

Old telephone directories make ideal personal address books. Simply cross out the names and addresses of people you don't know.

The Geordie was dying. On his deathbed, he looked up and said: "Is my wife here?"

His wife replies: "Yes, dear, I'm here, next to you."

The Geordie goes: "Are my children here?"

"Yes, daddy, we are all here," say the children.

The Geordie: "Are my other relatives also here?"

And they say: "Yes, we are all here..."

The Geordie rears up in bed and says: "Then why is the light on in the kitchen?"

A Geordie took a girl for a journey in a taxi. She was so beautiful he could hardly keep his eye on the meter.

Double glazing is doing great business in Newcastle and saving people a fortune. The kids can't hear the ice cream van when it comes round.

Three Geordieunians were in church one Sunday morning when the minister made a strong appeal for some very worthy cause, hoping that everyone in the congregation would give at least £10 or more. The three Geordies became very nervous as the collection plate neared them, and then one of them fainted and the other two carried him out.

A Mackem was hopelessly lost in the hinterlands of Newcastle and wandered about for days, ending up in Blakelaw. Finally he caught the eye of an inhabitant, not always easy in Blakelaw. "Thank heaven I've met someone," he cried. "I've been lost for ages."

"Is there a reward out for you?" asked the Geordie.

"No," said the Mackem.

"Then you're still lost," was the reply.

Did you hear about the last wish of the henpecked husband of a houseproud Geordie wife? He asked to have his ashes scattered on the carpet.

A Geordie was ill with measles. "Send for my creditors," he said. "At last I can give them something."

Did you hear about the Geordie burglars who were arrested after a smash and grab raid?

They went back for the brick.

A Mackem was being tried for being drunk and disorderly. The judge asked him where he had bought the bottle of vodka.

"I didn't buy it, Your Honour," said the Mackem.

"A Geordie gave it to me."

"Fourteen days for perjury," said the judge.

Sunderland Magistrates Court Judge: "You are charged with throwing the Geordie out of the third floor window."

Jimmy: "It was my Mackem temper. I did it without thinking."

Judge: "Yes, I understand that, but don't you see how dangerous it might have been for anyone on the street below?"

"I have a very unusual Sunderland watch to offer you. It never needs a battery or any winding. It has no hands, and no face of any kind."

"But how can you tell the time?"

"That's easy. Ask anybody."

What's the difference between a Geordie and a coconut?

You can get a drink out of a coconut.

"Did anybody drop a roll of notes with an elastic band around them?" asked the Mackem voice.

"Yes, I did," said several eager voices in the Newcastle bank queue.

"Well," said the Mackem, "I just found the elastic band."

You can always tell a Geordie, but you can't tell him much.

Mackem tourist: "This seems like a very dangerous cliff. It's a wonder they don't put up a warning sign."

Geordie: "Yes, it is dangerous, but they kept a warning sign up for two years and no one fell over, so it was taken down."

Why are 50p pieces the shape they are?

So you can use a spanner to get them off a Geordie.

How do you tell you are in a Newcastle restaurant?

There's a fork in the sugar bowl.

The Geordie put a penny in a weighing machine. A card came out which said, "You are a friendly spend-thrift."

It got his weight wrong too.

Mackem insults about dumb Geordies:

He's got the full six-pack, but not the plastic thingy to hold it all together.

A gross ignoramus: 144 times worse than an ordinary ignoramus.

He's an ignoranus – an ignorant arsehole.

He's got a photographic memory, but no lens.

He donated his brain to science before he was finished using it.

He fell out of his family tree.

The gates are shut, the lights are flashing, but the train isn't coming.

He has two brains; one is lost and the other is out looking for it.

If brains were taxed, he'd get a rebate.

14

NEIGHBOURS

A Mackem and a Geordie lived next door to each other. The Mackem owned a hen and each morning would look in his garden and pick up one of his hen's eggs for breakfast. One day he looked out and saw that the hen had laid an egg in the Geordie's garden.

He was about to go next door when he saw the Geordie pick up the egg. The Mackem ran up to the Geordie and told him that the egg belonged to him because he owned the hen. The Geordie disagreed because the egg was laid on his property.

Anyway, they argued for a while until finally the Mackem smiled in that frightening way that they have and said: "In Sunderland we normally solve disputes by the following actions. I kick you in the groin and time how long it takes you to get back up, then you kick me in the groin and time how long it takes for me to get up. Whoever gets up quicker wins the egg."

The Geordie agreed to this and so the Mackem found his heaviest pair of boots and put them on. He took a few steps back, then ran toward the Geordie and kicked him as hard as he could in the balls.

The Geordie fell to the ground clutching his testicles, howling in agony for thirty minutes. Eventually he stood up and said: "Now it's my turn to kick you."

At this the Mackem said: "You just keep the egg."

The neighbour above was in the garden filling in a hole when his Geordie neighbour peered over the fence. Interested in what the man was up to, he politely asked: "What are you doing there?"

"My goldfish died," replied the Mackem without looking up, "and I've just buried him."

The neighbour was very concerned. "That's an awfully big hole for a goldfish, isn't it?"

The Mackem patted down the last heap of dirt then replied: "That's because he's inside your fucking cat."

In Newcastle lived a rich cat which was a bit of a snob, though she did deign to chat on occasion with her neighbour, a bin-raking tomcat from Sunderland. One day, she announced that she was about to have an operation, but she didn't mention what it was for.

Two weeks later, the Mackem cat saw her again and inquired as delicately as he could how she was feeling, then dared to ask what kind of operation she had had.

"Oh, I am quite well now, thank you," the Geordie cat replied, stiffly. "I had a hysterectomy."

"For God's sake!" the other cat exclaimed in exasperation. "Can you not just call a spayed a spayed."

15

ARCHITECTS

How many architects does it take to change a light bulb?

Architect's answer: Does it have to be a light bulb?

Newcastle answer: Does it have to be an architect?

Sunderland answer: It's not those fuckers who built the Metro, is it?

"Any complaints?" asked the prison governor of the jailed Mackem architect.

"Aye," replied Jimmy, "the walls are not built to scale."

16

BANTER

Sunderland taxi driver's comment comparing the robustness of supermarket carrier bags: "FOUR bottles of booze in one Lidl bag! You're walking on eggshells, man."

Mackem to Geordie: "Why is your beer like shagging in a canoe?"

Geordie: "Don't know, why?"

Mackem: "It's fucking close to water!"

The Mackem beggar in Newcastle Central Station shambled over, holding out his filthy hand, and said: "Give a poor old blind man a pound, man."

"But you can see out of one eye, I can see you doing it," said the Geordie.

"Everybody's a fucking critic, but let's be fair," said the Mackem, "gimme 50p."

A Mackem was recently flying to London. He decided to strike up a conversation with his seatmate.

"I've got a great Geordie joke. Would you like to hear it?"

"I should let you know first that I am actually from Newcastle."

"That's OK. I'll tell it really slowly."

So I was getting into my car, and this Geordie says to me: "Can you give me a lift?"

So I said, "Aye, sure. You look great, the world's your oyster, go for it."

Phone answering machine message in your chav estate of choice in Newcastle (and it is a wide choice): "If you don't need to buy smack and it is just dope you want, press the hash key."

Newcastle . . . because the Devil wanted a hell on earth.

If you want to get served quickly in a Newcastle pub, learn to be polite. In Polish.

The token Mackem woman is at the office night out in one of the few properly grungy bars left in

Newcastle. She is very attractive and has had a few. She gestures alluringly to the barman, who comes over immediately. When he arrives, she seductively signals that he should bring his face closer to hers. When he does so, she begins to gently caress his full beard, one of those annoying square-ended ones affected by Geordies, who think that it makes a difference.

"Are you the manager?" she asks, softly stroking his face with both hands.

"Actually, no," the man replies.

"Can you get him for me? I need to speak to him," she says, running her hands beyond his beard and into his hair.

"I'm afraid I can't," breathes the barman. "Is there anything I can do?"

"Yes, there is. I need you to give him a message," she continues, slyly popping a couple of her fingers into his mouth and allowing him to suck them gently.

"What should I tell him?" the bartender manages to say. "Please tell him," she whispers, "that there is no soap, toilet paper or towels in the ladies'."

As Donald the Geordie and Jimmy the Mackem were coming out of the pub one afternoon, it started to rain very heavily. "Do you think it will stop?" asked Donald.

"It always has," answered Jimmy.

A Mackem goes into a pub in Newcastle and says, "Quick, gizza a beer before the trouble starts!" The barman looks around the sleepy pub, shrugs and hands the man a pint. The Mackem quaffs it immediately. "Quick! Gizza another beer before the trouble starts!" The barman looks at him oddly but pours him another pint. He again downs it immediately. "Quick, another one before the trouble starts!" The barman draws him another beer, with a frown on his face, and hands it over reluctantly. Again, the Mackem drinks it fast. "Quick, another beer before the trouble starts!" The barman exasperatedly asks: "Look, exactly what trouble are you talking about?"

The Mackem says: "I'm skint!"

A new Mackem version of the classic:

Do, a beer, a Mexican beer.
Ray, a man who buys me beer.
Mi, I'd like to have a beer.
Fa, a long, long way for beer.
So, I think I'll have a beer.
La, la, la, la, la, la, beer!
Ti, no thanks, I'll have a beer.
And that brings us back to Do!

17

GOLF

It is now generally accepted that golf did not originate in Newcastle. No Geordie would invent a game in which it was possible to lose a ball.

After the first hole, the Geordie turned to his Mackem opponent. "How many did you take?" he asked.

"Eight," replied the Mackem.

"I took seven, so that's my hole," said the Geordie. After the second hole, the Geordie asked the same question. This time the Mackem shook his head. "Ha'way, man," he replied, "it's my turn to ask first."

A Geordie golf pro, after ten years of retirement, went back to the game. He'd found his ball.

18

FOOTBALL

A new blue and white Oxo cube is about to be launched in the shops in both Sunderland and Newcastle to recognise the achievements of both Everton and Man City. It will be called 'laughing stock'.

What do you sing to a Geordie taking a bath?
Happy Birthday To You.

A 22-year-old secretary from Sunderland was on holiday in Miami. However, as she walked along the beach eyeing the big-bosomed girls walking arm-in-arm with their boyfriends, she became distraught, for she had a rather insignificant bosom herself. Suddenly, she spied a murky old bottle that had washed up on the beach, and for want of alternative amusement, picked it up. Poof! (Yes, they have them in Miami) Out comes a genie, complete with flowing oriental robes, and immediately offered to grant her any two of anything that she desired.

"Give me a pair of the biggest tits in the whole, wide world," she moaned. Poof! Poof! (yes, two of them) Immediately there emerged, before her very eyes, Keegan and Shearer.

A Mackem walked into a pub with a dog under his arm, just in time to hear the Saturday afternoon footie results on the telly.

"Sunderland three, Newcastle nil," said the announcer, at which point the guy shouted: "A'reet!" and the dog shouted: "Ah nah" and started bawling his head off.

More than astonished, the barman leaned over the counter and said: "Eh, your dog just shouted 'Oh no!'"

"I know," said the dog's owner. "He always does that when Newcastle lose."

"What does he do when they win?" asked the barman.

"I don't know," said the Mackem, with an evil smile, "I've only had him for a year and a half."

The same guy an hour or so later was waxing nostalgic about a previous pet: "My dog watched all the games. When Sunderland won it jumped up and down and clapped its little paws. When we lost it used to do somersaults."

"You're kiddin, man. How many somersaults?" asked the impressed barman.

The Mackem replied: "Depended how hard I kicked it."

A man, out walking his dog in a Newcastle street, came across an old bottle from which a genie appeared, offering the man a wish. (The usual way with bottles and genies in Newcastle. In Sunderland you get three wishes). Startled, the man asks if his dog could win at Crufts. The genie looks at the flea-bitten, limping dog and replies, "I'm not a miracle worker. Think of another wish." The man then asks: "Can you get United to win the Cup?" The genie immediately says, "Let me have another look at your dog."

Sunderland's kit for next season has just been unveiled. It's all-white with a pointed white hood and a flaming cross on the front.

And a tasteful little tribute to a former manager:

There's only one Bobby Robson
There's only one Bobby Robson
With his walking stick
And his zimmerframe
Bobby Robson's pissed himself again

19

EARTHQUAKE HITS NEWCASTLE

A NUMBER OF MAJOR EARTHQUAKES MEASURING 3.2 ON THE RICHTER SCALE, HIT IN THE EARLY HOURS OF MONDAY 21ST OCTOBER 2008 EPICENTERED ON NEWCASTLE, UK

Victims can be seen wandering aimlessly with relatives, muttering: "How man mutha man. Gan canny or we'll dunsh summick." Several were heard to say: "Eeeh man, ahm gannin te the booza. Ye knaa what ah mean leik? Whees i' the netty?"

They also said (many times) "Fuck" and "Some gadgie's just knacked me 'ouse." The earthquake decimated the area, causing approximately £10 worth of damage. Subsequent to the seismic activity, some fireworks missed their intended human targets, causing damage to nearby historic and scientifically significant litter. It is estimated that, during the confusion, over £5 million worth of robbery-time was lost, damaging the Geordieunian economy.

Many were woken well before their giro arrived. Thousands are confused and bewildered, trying to come to terms with the fact that something interesting has happened in Newcastle. One resident, Donna-Marie Dutton, a 17-year-old mother-of-three said: "It felt just like when the Toon Army came round one night. Little Chantal-Leanne came running into my bedroom shouting: 'Fuck'. My youngest two, Liam-Noel and Kevin slept through it. I was still shaking when I was watching Trisha the next morning."

Apparently, though, looting did carry on as normal. The British Red Cross have so far managed to ship 4000 crates of Newky Broon to the area to help the stricken masses. Rescue workers are still searching through the rubble and have found large quantities of personal belongings including fireworks, Burberry caps, benefit books and jewellery from Elizabeth Duke at Argos.

HOW YOU CAN HELP: This appeal is to raise clothing and food parcels for those unfortunate enough to be caught up in it. Clothing is most sought after. Items required include: caps, Adidas tracksuit bottoms, white socks, shell suits & boots.

Food parcels may be harder to put together but necessary all the same. Required foodstuffs include: pies, chips, McDonalds, Newky Broon & fireworks.

Geordieunians have insisted: "to avoid problems with the social and tax authorities (translation: they don't need any more handouts but just wish to be able to "help themselves" in this difficult time), more than the just dole money they already claim (for five different people). £10 can provide a hammer, which can be used to batter grannies and back up shoplifting exploits, providing enough money to support a family of Geordies on McDonalds for the foreseeable future. £5 will provide a Geordieunian with essential E's and scag, 22p buys a biro for filling in a spurious compensation claim. If you can afford it, £120 buys a new pair of Nike Airs, justifying the chavs' decision to tuck their tracksuit bottoms into their socks, and helping said individual to avoid being caught while nicking said trainers from JD Sports.

Please do not send money directly to Geordieunians, as there is a good chance they'll come looking for you, realising in their primitive way, that where there is money to give away, there is great potential for robbery.

Please give generously. We know where you live.

20

CINDERELLA

Mackem quick thinking (and a true story).

At Halloween a teenager in one of the nicer parts of Sunderland (not telling) was reported by a curtain twitcher to be having sexual congress with a pumpkin in a front garden.

Here's the policewoman's account of what happened when she approached the young man.

"He was holding the pumpkin against the wall and I just went up and said, 'Excuse me, but you do realize that you are having sex with a pumpkin?'"

He froze and was clearly very surprised that I was there and then looked me straight in the face and said: "A pumpkin? Christ . . . is it midnight already?"

21

GEORDIES AND SEX

An elderly man was walking through the French countryside, admiring the beautiful spring day, when over a hedgerow he spotted a young couple making love in a field. Getting over his initial shock, he said to himself: "Ah, young love . . . ze spring time, ze air, ze flowers . . . C'est magnifique!" and continued to watch, remembering good times.

Suddenly he drew in a breath and said: "Mais . . . Sacre bleu! Ze woman – she is dead!" and he hurried along as fast as he could to the town to tell Jean, the police chief. He came, out of breath, to the police station and shouted: "Jean . . . Jean zere is zis man, zis woman . . . naked in farmer Gaston's field making love."

The police chief smiled and said: "Come, come, Henri. You are not so old; remember ze young love, ze spring time, ze air, ze flowers? Ah, l'amour! Zis is okay."

"Mais non! You do not understand; ze woman, she is dead!"

Hearing this, Jean leapt up from his seat, rushed out of the station, jumped on his bike, pedalled down to the field, confirmed Henri's story, and pedalled all the way back non-stop to call the doctor.

"Pierre, Pierre . . . this is Jean, I was in Gaston's field; zere is a young couple naked 'aving sex."

To which Pierre replied: "Jean, I am a man of science. You must remember, it is spring, ze air, ze flowers, Ah, l'amour! Zis is very natural."

Jean, still out of breath, gasped in reply, "NON, you do not understand; ze woman, she is dead!"

Hearing this, Pierre exclaimed: "Mon Dieu!" grabbed his black medicine bag, stuffed in his thermometer, stethoscope, and other tools, jumped in the car and drove like a madman down to Gaston's field. After carefully examining the participants he drove calmly back to Henri and Jean, who were waiting at the station.

He got there, went inside, smiled patiently, and said: "Ah, mes amis, do not worry. Ze woman, she is not dead, she is from Newcastle."

After having their tenth child, and finally finding out why this was happening, a couple from Sunderland decided that enough was enough. The husband went to his doctor and told him that he and his wife didn't want to have any more children. The doctor told him that there was a procedure called a vasectomy that could fix the problem. The doctor told the man that he was to go home, get a firework, put it in a can, then hold the can up to his ear and count to ten. The Mackem said to the doctor, "I may not be the smartest man, but I don't see how putting a banger in a can next to my ear is going to help me." So, the couple drove to Newcastle to get a second opinion. The doctor was just about to tell them about the procedure for a vasectomy when he noticed they were from Sunderland. This doctor also told the man to go home and get a banger, place it in a tin can, hold it next to his ear and count to ten.

Figuring that both doctors couldn't be wrong, the man went home, lit a firework and put it in a can. He held the can up to his ear and began to count, "1, 2, 3, 4, 5 . . ." at which point he paused, placed the can between his legs and resumed counting on his other hand . . .

A young Geordie was all set up for his very first sexual experience, but his girlfriend says: "Sorry Freddy, not without a condom." He is totally skint and walking disconsolately around, knowing better than to ask anyone in Newcastle for money, when he eventually meets Old Jess, a very good friend of his father.

Young Freddy explains his problem and is told in return: "Don't worry son, I can help you out." He vanishes for a moment and returns with a condom.

Freddy takes off and the night is beyond his wildest expectations. A week later, he meets Old Jess in the street and tells him about his experience.

"It was wonderful, Jess. Thanks to you, I had the best time I have ever had."

"Just glad I could help out, son; now where's the condom?" asked Old Jess.

Freddy looks at him and replies: "I threw it away."

Old Jess, with a scowl on his face says, "Ah, you are in trouble now, boy. That condom belonged to the club."

22

NUTTY STORIES

A Mackem in Newcastle for the footie goes into a restaurant and orders a carry-out. While he waits, he grabs a handful of peanuts from the bowl on the counter, and as he starts to chew he hears a voice say: "That's a beautiful shirt, is that silk? Very nice choice!"

Wondering who made the comment, and mindful of all the advice he has had regarding Geordies' sexual proclivities, he looks around and doesn't see anyone nearby who could be speaking to him. With a shrug, he pops a few more peanuts into his mouth. Next he hears the voice say: "That is a lovely pair of shoes, bonny lad. Are they Italian leather? They look great!"

A little worried, the man decides to move away and play the slot machine. As he puts a coin in the one-armed bandit he hears a harsh voice say: "You ugly Mackem prick." He looks around but there's still no-one there. A couple of seconds later the second voice says: "Fuck off, you smelly Sunderland tosser!"

At this, the man called the barman in the restaurant over. "Hey, I must be goin' off my head," he told the barman. "I keep hearing these voices, one saying poofy things, and one noising me up, and there's not a soul in here but us. If you are a ventriloquist, you are dead."

"Ho'way man, no," answered the barman. "That's the peanuts . . . they're complimentary, but the bandit's well out of order."

A Geordie in his mid-forties goes looking for a job on a building site in Sunderland. On meeting the foreman, he enquires about any vacancies he may have. "Aye, well, I've just had to let someone go, so I'm a man down. Do you have any experience?"

The man pauses and looks anxious before telling him of his work history.

"Well, you see, I've been involved in major construction work all my life, but I was involved in an accident a couple of years ago and haven't worked since."

"What happened?" the foreman enquired.

"Well, to cut a long story short, I was working with a large industrial saw when it slipped and . . . unfortunately, I castrated myself."

"Ouch!" the foreman said, wincing at the thought

and studiously avoiding jokes about Geordies having no balls anyway. "Right, you obviously have loads of experience otherwise, so come down tomorrow morning at nine and I'll get you started."

"That's great," said the man, "but don't you and your crew start work at eight?"

The foreman nods and, with a very Mackem grin says: "Aye, but we just stand about scratching our balls for the first hour."

A Geordie and a Mackem were sitting next to each other on an aeroplane. The Geordie leans over to the Mackem and asks if he wants to play a game. The Mackem just wants to sleep so he politely declines, turns away and tries to sleep. The Geordie persists and explains that it's a really easy game. He explains: "I ask a question and if you don't know the answer you pay me £5. Then you ask a question and if I don't know the answer I'll pay you £5." Again the Mackem politely declines and tries to sleep.

The Geordie, now somewhat agitated, says: "OK, if you don't know the answer you pay me £5 and if I don't know the answer I pay you £50!" That got the Mackem's attention, so he agrees to the game. The Geordie asks the first question: "What's the distance from the earth to the moon?" The Mackem doesn't say a word and just hands the Geordie £5.

Now, it's the Mackem's turn. He asks the Geordie: "What goes up a hill with three legs and comes down on four?" The Geordie looks at him with a puzzled look, takes out his laptop, looks through all his references and after about an hour wakes the Mackem and hands the Mackem £50. The Mackem politely takes the £50, turns away, and tries to return to sleep.

The Geordie, a little miffed, asks: "Well, what's the answer to the question?" Without a word, the Mackem reaches into his wallet, hands £5 to the Geordie, turns away, and returns to sleep.

A Mackem and a Geordie were stopped by the police for being drunk and disorderly. It turned out that the first had been drinking battery acid and the second had been swallowing fireworks.

The Mackem was charged and the Geordie was let off. The desk sergeant got a rocket for not prosecuting him.

23

SUNDERLAND ETIQUETTE

A Mackem pupil told his registration teacher that he would not be in on Friday because he was going to his sister's wedding. When he returned the following Monday the teacher asked him how it had gone. He also remembered that the boy's father was dead and asked him if he had given the bride away. The latter replied: "I could have, but I kept my mouth shut. I grass no-one."

Real quote from a Sunderland policeman:

"Relax, the handcuffs are tight because they're new. They'll stretch after you wear them for a while."

In Newcastle a true friend will pay the bail to get you out of jail. In Sunderland a true friend will be sitting beside you in jail saying: "We fucked that up, man."

24

LITTLE DARLINGS

At Cherrylaurellaburnum Primary, in one of the nicer parts of Newcastle, Miss Fotheringill is asking the good little boys and girls of primary two what their fathers do, so that the headmistress can mark out the future prefects. "My daddy is a judge, Miss Fotheringill," says little Samantha, brushing back the royal blue bow which holds her mane of freshly-washed blonde locks.

"Very good, Samantha dear," says Miss Fotheringill, placing a discreet tick beside little Samantha's name in her big black book before moving on to the desk of little Roland.

"My daddy's a consultant surgeon, Miss Fotheringill," says little Roland, his big blue eyes filled with the innocence of freshly cut church lawns.

"That's very nice, Roland dear," says Miss Fotheringill, marking little Roland down as a future head boy and moving on to the desk of little Jimmy, whose father was a Sunderland bookie who won the lottery and whose mother is a poisoner. Miss

Fotheringill does not know this, but the tattoos of swallows flitting across little Jimmy's neck and up under his ear has already drawn her to the conclusion that little Jimmy is definitely not future officer material. Nevertheless, she asks the same question of him.

"My dad's dead," says little Jimmy.

"Oh dear," says Miss Fotheringill, overcome with remorse for her unkind thoughts about the poor lad. "And what did he do before he died, little James?"

"He grabbed his throat and went 'Aaaarrrrggghhhh', Miss."

25

DEAD GEORDIES. THERE AREN'T ENOUGH OF THEM

A Geordie went to live in Sunderland but unfortunately (kind of) he died. Two Mackems went around from house to house collecting money to give him a decent funeral.

"Excuse me," they asked up one close, "would you contribute even just 50 pence to bury a Newcastle man?"

"Yeh," said the Mackem, "here's £10 – bury twenty of them."

A Geordie woke up one morning to find his wife cold and stiff beside him. And she was dead as well. He jumped from his bed and ran, horror-stricken, into the kitchen. "Marisa," he said breathlessly to the au pair. "Si, si," she cried. "What is it? Que pasa?"

"Just one egg for breakfast this morning."

The insurance man knocked lightly on the door of the Newcastle semi-detached. The widower, his black suit contrasting with his pale white features, opened it very slowly. He ushered the insurance man into the living room, where two (very small) glasses of sherry were poured. They sat in silence until the insurance man dug into his briefcase and then in a very quiet voice said: "Everything is in order, Mr Donald. Here is our cheque for £500,000."

Donald stared at the cheque: "Five hundred thousand," he muttered. "Five hundred thousand pounds for a life of goodness, love, faith, devotion and charity. You know –" (and here he stopped to wipe away a tear) "I'd gladly give half of this back to have Margaret alive today."

A Mackem stopped before a grave in a Newcastle cemetery, containing a tombstone declaring: "Here lies a Newcastle lawyer and an honest man."

"And who would ever think," he murmured, "there would be room enough for two men in that one small grave."

26

MACKEM ATTITUDES TO BOOZE

And God said: "Let there be vodka!" And He saw that it was good and partook mightily. Then God said: "Let there be light!" And then He said: " 'Old on, 'old on – too much light."

To some it is just a bottle of Buckfast. To some Geordies it is an entire Social Work Department.

The problem with Newcastle people is that when they aren't drunk, they're sober.

Time is never wasted when you're wasted all the time.

Sunderland saying: "24 hours in a day, 24 bottles in a case. Coincidence?"

Life is a waste of time, time is a waste of life, so get wasted all of the time and have the time of your life.

Reality is an illusion that occurs due to lack of alcohol.

If I had all the money I've spent on booze . . . I'd spend it on booze.

Buckfast is proof that God loves us and wants us to be happy.

The problem with Geordies is that they always seem to be a few drinks behind.

Give me a woman who loves beer and I will conquer the world.

You're not drunk if you can lie on the floor without holding on.

You know you're drunk when you fall off the floor.

And, as Tom Waits so memorably said for most Mackems: "I'd rather have a bottle in front of me than a frontal lobotomy."

27

IT'S THE ACCENT

A young Mackem woman was on her first Mediterranean cruise and was talking to a Geordie matron who somewhat snobbishly announced that she had been on many, concluding by saying in that whiny Geordie way: "My Peter works for Cunard." The Mackem looked at her and said: "This might just be our first cruise, but my man works fuckin' 'ard as well."

28

A WORD TO THE WISE

An old Mackem is wandering about Newcastle city centre for ages looking for a friendly face and a place for a bite that doesn't take a mortgage to fund. He sees a young barman having a fag outside a pub and the young guy gives him a friendly smile and a nod, as he is a Mackem too. Delighted, the old guy goes into the pub and is served by the young guy. The pensioner asks for a bowl of soup and smiles up at the young guy and says: "And maybe a kind word as well, man?"

The young guy brings the soup and as he is turning away the old guy catches his sleeve and says: "And the kind word?" The young Mackem leans over and whispers in his ear: "Don't eat the soup."

29

SILLY, BUT NOT STUPID

There was a Mackem living in Newcastle who always hung around a supermarket owned by a Geordie. The owner, Tim, doesn't know what Jimmy's problem is, but the local boys like to tease him. They say he is two bricks shy of a load, or two pickles short of a ploughman's lunch. To prove it, sometimes they offer Jimmy his choice between a pound and a fifty pence piece. He always takes the fifty pence, they say, because it's bigger. One day after Jimmy grabbed the fifty pence piece, Tim got him off to one side and said, "Those boys are making you out to be a fool. They think you don't know the pound is worth more than the 50p. Are you grabbing the 50p because it's bigger, or what?" Jimmy said, "Well, if I took the £1, they'd stop doing it, wouldn't they?"

30

ACCIDENTS

A Mackem and a Geordie were travelling on a motorcycle through windy countryside. When it became too breezy for one of them, he stopped and put his overcoat on backward to keep the wind from ballooning it away from him. A few miles further down the road, the motorcycle hit a tree, killing the driver and stunning the man with the reversed coat. Later, when the Superintendent visited the scene, he said to the policeman standing nearby: "What happened?"

"Well," the young policeman replied, "one of them was dead when I got here, and by the time I got the head of the lad from Newcastle straightened out, he was dead too."

A Geordie lawyer opened the door of his BMW, when suddenly a car came along and hit the door, ripping it off completely.

When the police arrived at the scene, the lawyer was complaining bitterly about the damage to his precious BMW.

"Officer, look what they've done to my Beeeeemer!" he whined.

"You lawyers are so materialistic, you make me sick," retorted the constable. "You're so worried about your stupid BMW that you didn't even notice that your arm was ripped off!"

"Oh no!" replied the lawyer, finally noticing the bloody right shoulder where his arm once was. "Where's my Rolex?"

31

PHILOSOPHY

A Geordie is a man who feels badly when he feels good for fear he'll feel worse when he feels better.

Showing-off is a hanging offence in Newcastle.

How many Geordies does it take to change a light bulb?
    None, they form a self-help group called: "How to cope with life in the dark."

Sunderland saying: Life is shite. Get a fucking helmet, okay?

To the Liverpudlian, the glass is half full.
    To the Cockney, the glass is half empty.
    To the Geordie, the glass is twice as big as it needs to be.

32

CANNIBALLOCKS

A Mackem, a Geordie and a Londoner were captured by cannibals. The chief comes to them and says: "The bad news is that now we've caught you, we're going to kill you. We will put you in a pot, cook you, eat you and then we're going to use your skins to build a canoe. The good news is that you can choose how to die."

The Geordie says: "Give me a case of gin and a few bottles of tonic." He then retires to his hut and after a few choruses of: "Magpies till I die!" drinks himself to death and is duly skinned, cooked, eaten, and turned into a canoe.

The Londoner says: "Brandy for me please, might as well go the expensive way. And a little ginger ale." The chief gives him the brandy and the mixer, and after a few renditions of: "Chelsea for ever!" duly expires and is skinned, cooked etc.

The Mackem says: "Gizza crate of vodka and a fork. No mixer necessary." The chief is puzzled, but he shrugs and gives him the vodka and the fork. The

Mackem takes them and goes to his hut. Later the chief goes to see him and there he is, half of the vodka gone, broken bottle in one hand, fork in the other, jabbing himself all over . . . the stomach, the sides, the chest, everywhere. There is blood gushing out, it's horrible. The chief is appalled and asks: "My God, what are you doing?"

And the Mackem responds, as he sticks the broken bottle in the chief's face: "Fuck you AND your canoe!"

33

THE LORD GOD AND GEORDIES

Eric the Geordie finds himself in dire trouble. His business has gone bust and he's got serious financial problems. He's so desperate that he decides to ask God for help. "God, please help me. I've lost my store and if I don't get some money, I'm going to lose my house too. Please let me win the lottery."

Lottery night. Someone else wins.

Eric prays again. "God, please let me win the lottery! I've lost my store, my house and I'm going to lose my car as well."

Lottery night again! Still no luck. Eric prays again.

"I've lost my business, my house and my car. My little ones are starving. I don't often ask You for help and I have always been a good servant to You. PLEASE just let me win the lottery this one time so I can get back on my feet!"

Suddenly there is a blinding flash as the heavens open and the voice of God Himself thunders, in a very Mackem accent: "Gizza break here, Eric.

Meet Me halfway, you miserable, moanin' Geordie gobshite. Buy a ticket!"

A Newcastle couple on their way to get married were tragically killed in a terrible crash. Upon presenting themselves to St. Peter at the gates to heaven, they asked if they could get married, specifying that they would like the ceremony carried out by a Geordie priest. "Give me some time," said St. Peter, "and I'll check."

They waited and waited. After several months, they asked again. "I'm working on it," said St. Peter.

Months turned into years, then decades. Finally, after 30 years, St. Peter came running to them. "OK, now you can get married!"

However, after a few months of married life, the couple really were not happy. They sought out St. Peter and asked if there were divorces in heaven.

"Are you serious? It took me 30 years to find a Newcastle priest up here. I'll NEVER find a lawyer!"

A rich Geordie lawyer was near death. He was very grieved because he had worked so hard stealing people's money and he wanted to be able to take it with him to heaven. So he began to pray that he might be able to take some of his wealth with him.

A Mackem angel hears his plea and appears to him. "Sorry, man, but you can't take your dosh with you." The man implores the angel to speak to God to see if He might bend the rules.

The man continues to pray that his wealth could follow him. The angel reappears and informs the man that God has decided to allow him to take one suitcase with him. Overjoyed, the man gathers his largest suitcase and fills it with pure gold bars and places it beside his bed.

Soon afterward the man dies and shows up at the gates of Heaven to greet St. Peter. St. Peter, who by sheer coincidence is also a Mackem, as is God, clocks the suitcase and says: "Hold on a minute, you can't bring that in here."

But, the man explains to St. Peter that he has permission and asks him to verify his story with the Lord. Sure enough, St. Peter checks and comes back saying: "You're right. You are allowed one carry-on bag, but I'm supposed to check its contents before letting it through."

St. Peter opens the suitcase to inspect the worldly goods that the man found too precious to leave behind and says in surprise: "You brought pavement?"

An evil atheist Geordie explorer in the deepest Amazon suddenly finds himself surrounded by a bloodthirsty group of natives. Upon surveying the situation, he says quietly to himself: "Oh God, I'm fucked."

There is a ray of light from heaven and a Mackem voice booms out: "No, evil atheist, you are NOT fucked. Pick up that stone at your feet and bash in the head of the chief standing in front of you."

So the explorer picks up the stone and proceeds to turn the chief's head to mince.

As he stands above the lifeless body, breathing heavily and surrounded by 100 natives with a look of shock on their faces, God's voice booms out again: "Right lad, NOW you're fucked."

34

OPPORTUNITIES

There was a Mackem, a Geordie and Sharon Stone sitting together in a train. Suddenly the train went through a tunnel and, as it was an old-style steam train, there were no lights in the carriages and it went completely dark. Then there was this kissing noise and the sound of a really loud slap. When the train came out of the tunnel, Sharon Stone and the Mackem were sitting as if nothing had happened and the Geordie had his hand against his face going: "Ouch!"

The Geordie was thinking: "The Mackem must have kissed Sharon Stone and she missed him and slapped me instead."

Sharon Stone was thinking: "The Geordie must have tried to kiss me and actually kissed the Mackem and got slapped for it."

And the Mackem was thinking: "This is great. The next time the train goes through a tunnel I'll make that kissing noise and slap that Geordie lad again."

A Mackem and a Geordie are strolling along Blackpool beach when they find a lamp. They clean it up and out pops a genie. "I'll give you each one wish (It's a Newcastle genie) for anything you want," says the genie.

The Geordie thinks then says. "I believe in Newcastle for the folk of Newcastle. I'm sick and tired of all these Mackems coming to MY city, driving property values down, laughing, drinking and winning at football. I wish for a huge wall around Newcastle to keep the Mackems out."

POOF! (It is still Newcastle) and it's done. The Mackem has a think. "Genie?" he says "tell me about this wall."

"Well," says the genie, "it's 500 feet high, a third of a mile thick, nothing can get in and nothing can get out."

"OK," says the Mackem. "Fill it with water."

A Mackem is walking along the beach when he discovers an old bottle. He takes the cork out of it and a genie appears.

The genie says: "I'll grant you three wishes (It is a Mackem genie), but whatever you wish for, the Geordies will receive double."

"Ok," says Jimmy. "My first wish is for a million pounds."

The genie says: "Ok, but the Geordies will receive two million."

"No problem," says the Mackem, "I can live with that."

"My second wish is that Sunderland win the Cup." Again, the genie says:

"That's fine, but United will win the next two after that."

The Mackem shakes his head but agrees: "Ok, I can live with that."

"What is your third wish?" asks the genie.

"Well," said the Mackem slowly, "I'd like to donate a kidney."

35

WHAT'S IN A NAME?

A Geordie and his partner were driving their fuck-off sized Recreational Vehicle and were nearing Sunderland. Justin said to Cammie: "It's pronounced Sunlun or something like that." Cammie demurred, a thing Newcastle lawyers do a lot of.

Since they were hungry, they pulled into a place to get something to eat. At the counter, Justin said to the waitress: "Cammie and I can't seem to be able to agree on how to pronounce this place. We're from Newcastle. Will you tell me where we are and say it very slowly so that I can understand."

The waitress looked at him and said: "Buuurrrgerrr Kiiiinnnng."

36

NEW SIMPLIFIED FORM FOR 2008/09 SUNDERLAND COUNCIL TAX

1. Calculate how much money you made in 2007.
2. Send it to us.

37

SUNDERLAND'S FINEST

On Christmas morning a policeman on horseback is heading for the major Christmas present resettlement area that is Pennywell. He is sitting at a traffic light and next to him is a little boy on a shiny new bike. The cop says to the kid, "Nice bike you've got there. Did Santa steal that for you?" The boy says, "Yes." The cop says, "Well, next year tell Santa to put a light on that bike." The cop then proceeds to issue the kid a bicycle safety order, meaning that he has to turn up at the police station. The boy takes the chit and before he rides off says, "By the way, that's a nice horse you've got there. Did Santa bring that to you?" Humouring the kid, the policeman says: "Yes, that he did." The boy says: "Well, next year tell Santa to put the prick underneath the horse."

Sunderland Police, MI5, and a secret Government department are all trying to prove that they are the best at apprehending criminals. The Prime Minister decides to give them a test. He releases a rabbit into a forest and each of them has to catch it.

MI5 goes in. They place animal informants throughout the forest. They question all plant and mineral witnesses. After three months of extensive investigations they conclude that rabbits do not exist.

The ultra-secret Government department goes in. After two weeks with no success they poison the forest with some mysterious substance, killing nearly everything in it, and they make no apologies. Nobody ever mentions their failure. Or their existence. A bit like Masons in the police force.

Sunderland's finest go in. They come out two hours later with a Rottweiler that is showing a bit of wear and tear. It is limping on all four legs and pissing blood, but there are of course no visible injuries.

The dog is yelling: "Okay! Okay! I'm a rabbit! I'm a rabbit!"

GEORDIES

VS

MACKEMS

Why Tyneside is better than Wearside

GEORDIES START HERE

First published 2008
by Black & White Publishing Ltd
29 Ocean Drive, Edinburgh EH6 6JL

1 3 5 7 9 10 8 6 4 2   08 09 10 11 12

ISBN: 978 1 84502 227 3

A CIP catalogue record for this book is available from the British Library.

Typeset by RefineCatch Ltd, Bungay, Suffolk
Printed and bound by Norhaven A/S, Denmark

INTRODUCTION

Every Geordie worth his or her salt knows that talk is cheap in Sunderland because supply exceeds demand and that the first question at a Sunderland pub quiz is: "What are you looking at?" but not many know why the River Wear runs through Sunderland. The answer being of course that if it walked it would get mugged.

It has been asserted that Mackems are so dense that light bends around them and if you stand close enough to one, not that one would want to, but if you do, you can hear the sea.

You may learn within that parents from Pennywell in Sunderland are incredibly hard, but they never smack their children. Well, maybe one or two grams to get them to sleep at night.

The song below is sung in Newcastle, and not just at football grounds. I've heard it sung in pubs late of an evening, when the beer is revealing the real feeling.

To the tune of 'You Are My Sunshine'

You're just a Mackem
A smelly Mackem
You're only happy on Giro day
Your Ma's a stealer
Your Da's a dealer
Please don't take my hubcaps away.

Geordies know that in Mackem families, father, mother and sister often don't add up to three, but that they do keep their knives sharp.

These are hard hits from the Geordie side, digs, pokes in the eye, sharp jibes and bludgeoning diatribes, but it's just friendly rivalry really. Not.

1

ATTITUDES AND INSULTS

A Geordie, a former public schoolboy, says that though he could buy a mansion in Sunderland and have a million or so left over by moving there, he wouldn't want to live in a city where, more often than not, the school uniform is wellies.

True tale from a Newcastle pavement cafe.

Geordie: "It's a real shame that those ETA terrorists are bombing the Mackems in Benidorm."

Mackem at next table: "But Geordies go to Benidorm as well."

Geordie: "Not during the Sunderland holidays we don't."

How do you know when you're staying in a hotel in Sunderland? When you call the receptionist and say "I've got a leak in my sink" and the response is "Aye, fine, go ahead."

In Newcastle, tables and chairs outside means a chance to have a seat and a chat over your coffee or beer. In Sunderland, it's an eviction.

On the train from Sunderland to Newcastle, a Mackem was berating the Geordie sitting across from him in the compartment. "You Geordies are too stuffy. You set yourselves apart too much. Look at me and my brothers and sisters. We have Italian blood, Russian blood, Jewish blood, Danish blood, and Swedish blood. What do you say to that?"

The Geordie replied, "Your mother sounds like a very sporting lady."

Before the last World Cup, a primary school teacher in Newcastle asks her pupils if they want to see England win it. The full class put their hands up except for one girl who says she wants Sweden, or Trinidad and Tobago to win. Anyone, in fact, but England. Amazed, the teacher asks why, "Well miss, my mum and dad are Scottish so I'm a Scottish fan too." The teacher replies: "You don't have to be a Scotland fan because your parents are. If your mum was a prostitute and dad was a junkie that stole and beat up innocent people you wouldn't be like that."

"No miss," the girl says, "that would make me a Mackem."

Two boys were playing football in the park when suddenly one of them is attacked by a Rottweiler.

Thinking quickly, his friend rips a plank of wood from a fence, forces it into the dog's collar and twists it, breaking the dog's neck.

All the while, a journalist from the *Evening Chronicle* who was taking a stroll through the park is watching. He rushes over, introduces himself and takes out his pad and pencil to start his story for the next edition. He writes: "Brave United fan saves friend from vicious animal!"

The boy interrupts: "But I'm not a United fan."

The reporter starts again: "Heroic Boro fan rescues friend from horrific attack!"

Again the boy interrupts: "But I'm not a Boro fan either."

"Who do you support then?" inquires the reporter.

"Sunderland," comes the reply.

So the reporter starts again:

"Mackem bastard murders family pet."

Your average Mackem is a sort of one-man or one-woman slum. Inside and out.

To the tune of Mistletoe and Wine

DREAMING OF A MACKEM CHRISTMAS . . .

Christmas time, drunkenness and crime,
Children playing – in filth and grime,
With cars on fire – and radios from them
Time to rejoice – in be-ing Mackem,
It's a time for stealing, a time for receiving,
Knock-off stuff – what a great feelin'
Why pay top dollar – you can nick it for free,
Just like our electricity, gas and TV

Christmas time, pissups all the time
Nicking fags – spirits and wine
Wearing-shell-suits and Nikees – all knocked off gear
It's great getting pissed – on someone else's beer
Its a time for drinkin' – six packs of Stella
That you got – from some dodgy fella
Christmas is sound – Christmas is best
God bless our dealer – and the DSS
Christmas time – time to joy-ride
Then go and visit – family inside
With Dad on a six stretch – and Sis up the duff
This City of Black Cats can get pretty rough

So next time you're driving – through Mackem-city
You may just know why – the streets look so shitty

So keep a sharp eye out – for those dodgy deals
If you park for two minutes, they're off with your
wheels

Newcastle saying: Laugh alone and the world thinks
you're an idiot.

Sean Connery was interviewed by Michael
Parkinson, and bragged that despite his 78 years of
age, he could still have sex five times a night. Kate
Adie, who was also a guest, looked intrigued. After
the show, Kate said: "Sean, if I'm not being too forward, I'd love to have sex with an older man. Let's go
back to my place."

So they go back to her place and have great sex.
Afterwards, Sean says, "If you think that was good,
let me shleep for half an hour, and we can have
even better shex. But while I'm shleeping, hold my
baws in your left hand and my wullie in your right
hand."

Kate looks a bit perplexed, but says, "Okay." He
sleeps for half an hour, awakens, and they have
even better sex. Then Sean says, "Kate, that was
wonderful. But if you let me shleep for an hour, we
can have the besht shex yet. But again, hold my
baws in your left hand, and my wullie in your right

hand." Kate is now used to the routine and complies. The results are mind blowing. It happens five times.

Once it's all over, and the cigarettes are lit, Kate asks, "Sean, tell me, does my holding your balls in my left hand and your willie in my right stimulate you while you are sleeping?"

Sean replies, "No, it's just that the lasht time I shlept with a Mackem, she shtole my wallet."

Sean Connery has fallen on hard times. All work has dried up and he's just sat at home twiddling his thumbs. Suddenly the phone ring and Sean answers it. It's his agent and Sean gets very excited.

The agent says, "Sean, I've got a job for you. Starts tomorrow, but you've got to get there early, for 10ish."

Sean frowns and replies, "10ish? But I haven't even got a racket."

Sunderland are to bid to host 2012 Olympics, removing it from London, as it is costing us a fortune and we are getting sod all from it – a bit like the government, really.

In an attempt to influence the members of the International Olympic Committee on their choice

of venue for the games the organisers of Sunderland's bid have drawn up an itinerary and schedule of events. A copy has been leaked and is reproduced below.

Opening Ceremony

The Olympic flame will be ignited by a petrol bomb thrown by a native of the city (probably from the Pennywell area), wearing the traditional costume of shell suit, baseball cap and balaclava mask. It will burn for the duration of the games in a large chip van situated on the roof of the stadium.

The Events

In previous Olympic games until 2008, Britain's competitors have not been particularly successful. In order to redress the balance, some of the events have been altered slightly to the advantage of local athletes:

100 Metres Sprint

Competitors will have to hold a video recorder and microwave oven (one under each arm) and on the sound of the starting pistol, a police dog will be released from a cage 10 yards behind the athletes.

100 Metres Hurdle
As above but with added obstacles (i.e. car bonnets, hedges, garden fences, walls etc.)

Hammer
Competitors may choose the type of hammer they wish to use (claw, sledge, etc). The winner will be the one who can cause the most grievous bodily harm to members of the public within the time allowed.

Fencing
Entrants will be asked to dispose of as much stolen silver and jewellery as possible in 5 minutes.

Shooting
A strong challenge is expected from the local men in this event. The first target will be a moving police car, the next a post office van and then a Securicor wages vehicle.

Boxing
Entry to the boxing will be restricted to husband and wife teams, and will take place on a Friday night. The husband will be given 15 pints of Stella, while the wife will be told not to make him any tea when he gets home. The bout will then commence.

Cycling Time Trials
Competitors will break into the University bike sheds and take an expensive mountain bike owned by some mummy's boy from the country on his first trip away from home. All against the clock.

Cycling Pursuit
As above but the bike will belong to a visiting member of the Australian rugby team who will witness the theft.

Modern Pentathlon
Amended to include mugging, breaking and entering, flashing, joy-riding and arson.

The Marathon
A safe route has yet to be decided, but competitors will be issued with bags full of litter which they will distribute on their way round the course.

Swimming
Competitors will be thrown into the Wear. The first three survivors back will decide the medals.

Men's 50km Walk
Unfortunately this event will have to be cancelled as

police cannot guarantee the safety of anyone walking the streets of Sunderland.

Closing Ceremony
Entertainment will include formation rave dancing by members of Sunderland Health in the Community anti-drug campaigners, synchronised rock throwing and music by the Back to Roker Park Band. The Olympic flame will be extinguished by someone dropping an old washing machine onto it from the top floor of the block of flats next to the stadium. The stadium will then be boarded up before the local athletes break into it and remove all the copper piping and the central heating boiler.

Jimmy the Mackem was awarded £10,000 for injuries received after a traffic accident and his wife got £2,000. A friend asked how badly injured his wife had been in the accident. He replied, "She wasn't hurt at all but I had the presence of mind to break her leg before the police arrived."

Mackems love animals. They taste great.

The Mackem got lost in thought. It was unfamiliar territory.

Some people have a photographic memory. Some Mackems just don't have film.

There's many a Sunderland man with the heart of a little child. They usually keep them in jars.

There are two theories about arguing with Mackems. Neither of them works.

Newcastle omelette: First, borrow four eggs.
Sunderland omelette: First, steal four eggs.

2

ARE YOU LIVING TOO CLOSE TO SUNDERLAND?

Below are some tell-tale signs:

1. Your spouse has a poster of Roy Keane smiling as a role model.

2. You let your twelve-year-old daughter smoke at the dinner table in front of her kids.

3. You've been married three times and still have the same in-laws.

4. You think that a woman is "out of your league" because she asks for a glass with her Buckfast.

5. The phrase, "Thunderbirds are go!" reminds you the off licence has just opened.

6. You wish your toilet at home could be as 'clean' as the one in the bus station.

7. Anyone in your family ever died right after saying, "Hey! Watch this."

8. You think Dom Perignon is a Mafia leader.

9. Your wife's hairdo was once ruined by a ceiling fan.

10. Your school had a students' creche.

11. One, or more, of your kids was born on a pub pool table.

12. One, or more, of your kids was conceived on a pub pool table.

13. Your back door coal bunker is ideal for the Rottweiler to raise its pups.

14. The trade-in value of your transit goes up and down, depending on how full the tank is.

15. You don't have to leave the house to put rubbish in the wheelie bin.

16. You once lit a match in the bathroom and the windows blew out.

17. You only need one more stamp on your card to get a freebie at "Tom's Tattoos."

18. You can't get married to your childhood sweetheart because of the current bestiality laws.

19. You think 'loading a dishwasher' means getting your wife drunk.

20. Your toilet paper has page numbers on it.

and finally . . .

21. The soundtrack on your wedding video ends with the loudhailer message: "THIS IS THE POLICE."

Santa Claus, the tooth fairy, an intelligent Mackem and an old drunk are walking down the street together when simultaneously they each spot a fifty pound note.
Who gets it?
The old drunk, of course. The other three are mythological.

A father takes his young son to the zoo where they are fascinated by the lions. "Daddy, Daddy, why is that lion licking his bum?" asks the boy.
"Son, that's because he has just eaten a Mackem and is trying to get rid of the taste."

Geordie to Mackem: "You are depriving some poor village of its idiot."

The purchasing agent of a big company was a stuffy old Geordie, but he gave an extensive order to a Mackem salesman. Although he had won the business in open competition, the salesman was grateful at being chosen and sought a way to show it.

He knew he daren't offer the buyer a commission and a gift of money, he thought, would be regarded by him as an insult. The man, he noticed, constantly smoked cigars. So the salesman slipped out to a cigar shop and bought a box of fifty of the finest Havanas the tobacconist had. The price for the fifty was £500, but it had been a really big order that he had won. He brought the box back and asked the buyer to accept it with his compliments.

The latter explained that it was against company policy for its buyers to accept presents of any sort from those with whom the concern did business. He was sorry, he said, but he could not take the cigars as a present, even though he felt sure his young friend had tendered them with the best of intentions and in absolute good faith.

The young Mackem had another idea:

"Well," he said, "I hate to throw these cigars away. They are no use to me – I don't even smoke cigarettes. I wonder if you would buy them from me? There's no harm in that, surely."

"What would you be asking for them?" inquired the Geordie.

"I'll sell the whole fifty to you for a fiver," stated the salesman.

The buyer lifted one of the cigars from the top row, smelled it, rolled it in his fingers and eyed it closely.

"Okay," he said, "at that price I'll take four boxes."

Newcastle threat: I'll wring your neck, you little Mackem bastard, but only if you wash it.

Roy Keane was looking to sign some new players to help Sunderland's title push, so he sent his chief scout to Iraq to search for some new talent. Sure enough, the scout finds an outstanding 18-year-old striker and immediately signs him on a 3-year deal.

On getting back to England, Keane takes one look at him in training and immediately puts him in the starting line up for the big away game against Everton.

The new lad is fantastic, he scores a hat trick and creates four more as Sunderland romp it 7–0. Ecstatic after the game, the young lad phones his mum to tell her the good news.

"Mum," he says, "I've just made my debut and had a great game. The team loves me, the fans love me and the press loves me, even them twats on the radio phone-in love me. Life is great!"

"Well," says his mum, "I'm glad life is great for you. Shall I tell you what happened to us today? Your Dad's been murdered in the street, your sister and I were raped and beaten in broad daylight, and your brother's joined a vicious gang of killers."

"Mum, I don't know what to say. I'm so sorry."

"Sorry?" she yells down the phone. "You're fucking sorry? It's your fucking fault we moved to Sunderland in the first place!"

Badge spotted in one of Sunderland's fine call centres: "I'm just working here until a good fast food job opens up."

How many Mackem flies does it take to screw in a light bulb?

Only two, but you have to wonder how the sneaky little bastards got in there.

How many Sunderland fans does it take to change a light bulb?

Seven – one to change it, five to moan about it and

the coach to say that if the ref had done his job in the first place the light bulb would never have gone out.

Mackem teachers are known to use the following translations for the remarks they make on pupils' report cards:

"A born leader" – Runs a protection racket

"Easy-going" – Bone idle

"Good progress" – You should have seen him a year ago

"Friendly" – Never shuts up

"Helpful" – A creep

"Reliable" – Informs on his friends

"Expresses himself confidently" – Impertinent

"Enjoys physical education" – A bully

"Does not accept authority easily" – Dad is in prison

"Often appears tired" – Stays up all night watching television

"A rather solitary child" – He smells

"Popular in the playground" – Sells pornography

Mackems are so lazy that they won't marry a woman till she's pregnant.

A Sunderland fan's wife gets on to the bus holding her 3-week-old baby. The bus driver says: "Hey pet,

your baby is the ugliest baby I've ever seen!" The woman pays her fare and goes off and sits up the back of the bus almost in tears. A man says to her "What's up, love?" She says: "The bus driver has just been very rude to me." The man replies: "Although you are a filthy Mackem, you shouldn't let him get away with that, I reckon you should go and say something. He is a public servant and he can't do that to you." She says: "I will then, I'm off."

The gadgie then says: "Do you want me to hold your monkey?"

Two Mackems standing on a cliff. One has two budgies on one shoulder, the other has a parrot on his. The first Mackem jumps and goes screaming through the air to land in a crumpled heap on the ground below.

Seconds later, his mate jumps. Halfway down, he pulls out a pistol and blows the parrot's head off, but to no avail, as he crashes in a heap next to his mate. First Mackem moans, then says to his mate: "This budgie-jumping is overrated."

His mate half-turns his broken neck and replies: "Aye, and the parrot-shooting isn't much better."

3

GEORDIES AND DRINK

John the Geordie reckoned he was a great judge of a glass of whisky – and a merciless executioner.

Sandy the Geordie was sitting at the bar drinking double whiskies in one gulp as fast as the barman could put them in front of him. He eventually explained that it was the only way he could drink them after a terrible accident. "What sort of accident?" asked the barman. "Terrible," said Sandy. "I knocked one over with my elbow."

The priest of a church in one of the more salubrious districts of Newcastle was preaching a strong sermon about the evils of drink, and kept telling the congregation not to imbibe too frequently. He concluded: "We'll not make this sermon too personal, but if a short, bald-headed chap who owns a chain of video shops, two restaurants and a pub, and is sitting in the corner of the east gallery pew, takes it to heart, then the Lord surely does work in mysterious ways."

4

JUST DESERTS

A Geordie and a Mackem are walking along a beach, when they see an old bottle.

The Mackem picks it up and takes out the cork.

Out pops a genie who says, "I am the genie with the light brown hair. I will grant you three wishes each."

Wish 1 – "OK then," the Mackem says, "I wish every person in Sunderland was female apart from me."

Wish 1 – "I'd like a Ferrari," says the Geordie.

Wish 2 – The Mackem, wanting better than the Geordie says, "I wish everyone in Europe was female apart from me."

Wish 2 – "I'd like a garage for my Ferrari," says the Geordie.

Final wish – "I wish everyone in the world was female apart from me," says the Mackem.

Final wish – "I wish the Mackem to be gay!" says the Geordie.

Newcastle prayer: "God bless Newcastle. And God, we've got to flit to Sunderland tomorrow. So, good-bye God."

5

THIEVING MACKEMS

If you see a Mackem on a bicycle, why should you never swerve to hit him?

It could be your bike.

A Geordie woman said that whenever someone from Newcastle wears something expensive, it looks old, and when a Mackem does so, it looks stolen.

What is the difference between Batman and a Mackem?

Batman can go out without robbin'.

What did the little Mackem boy get for Christmas?

Your bike.

6

TERRACING TALK

We're Geordies, we're insane,
We drink Broon and sniff cocaine,
With a nick knack paddy wack give the dog a
 bone,
Why don't Sunderland fuck off home?

To the tune of 'Hey Baby'

Heeeey Mackems! Ooh ah,
I wanna kno-oo-oo-ow where's my video . . .
and my stereo and my dvd . . .
And my granny's purse.

7

STUPID MACKEMS

A scientist is researching the effects of the loss of brain power on people's speech. So he brings in a guy off the street to participate in the experiments.

As they attach the electrodes to his head, the guy says, "May I please have a drink of water?"

But the scientist ignores him and says to his assistant, "Remove 25 per cent of his brain power now."

The assistant does this and the guy then says, "Give me water."

Again the scientist ignores him and says, "Remove another 25 per cent."

Guy: "Give drink water."

Scientist: "Now another 25 per cent."

Guy: "Wawa, wawa."

Scientist: "And now, the final 25 per cent."

Guy (singing): "Come on Sunderland . . ."

A Mackem was out for a walk and came to a river and saw a Geordie on the opposite bank. "Hello there," she shouts, "how can I get to the other side?" The Mackem looked up the river, then down the

river, then shouted back, "You ARE on the other side."

The young Mackem's report card said: "At last some good news. We thought Wayne had reached rock bottom. But now he has developed a hitherto unsuspected talent for digging."

8

GEORDIE PHILOSOPHY

Newcastle question: If you try to fail, and succeed, which have you done?

In Newcastle they say: "Opportunities are never lost; someone will always take the one you missed." In Sunderland they say: "Do you mean oppurchancities?"

A closed mouth gathers no feet, as they say in Newcastle.

Newcastle saying: Give me ambiguity or give me something else.

The Geordies way of saying: "No," is to start a conservation group.

9

HEAVEN

"Heaven seems not all that much better than Sunderland," a Mackem is said to have confided, after death, to a friend who had died before him. "Bonny lad, this isn't Heaven," replied his pal.

A man from Newcastle, a Scouser and a Mackem wound up together at the Pearly Gates. St. Peter informed them that in order to get into Heaven, they would each have to answer one question.

St. Peter addressed the Geordie and asked, "What was the name of the ship that crashed into the iceberg?" He answered quickly, "That would be the Titanic." St. Peter let him through the gate.

St. Peter turned to the Scouser and, thinking that Heaven didn't need all the attitudes that this guy would bring with him, decided to make the question a little harder: "How many people died on the ship?" Fortunately for him, he had seen the movie and answered, "About 1,500."

"That's right! You may enter."

St. Peter then turned to the Mackem. "Name them."

10

HELL

A Geordie, a Mackem and a Scouser found themselves in hell. They were a little confused at their situation, and they were startled to see a door in the wall open. Behind the door was perhaps the ugliest woman they had ever seen.

She was 3'4' dirty, and you could smell her even over the brimstone.

The voice of the Devil was heard: "Scouser, you have sinned! You are condemned to spend the rest of eternity in bed with this woman!"

He was then whisked through the door by a group of lesser demons to his torment.

This understandably shook up the other two, and so they both jumped when a second door opened, and they saw an even more disgusting example of womanhood gone wrong. She was over 7' tall, monstrous, covered in thick black hair, and flies circled her.

The voice of the Devil was heard: "Geordie, you have sinned! You are condemned to spend the rest of eternity in bed with this woman!" And he too was whisked off.

The Mackem now alone, felt understandably anxious, and feared the worst when the third door opened. As it inched open, he strained to see the figure of . . . Paris Hilton.

Delighted, the Mackem jumped up, taking in the sight of this beautiful woman, barely dressed in a skimpy bikini. Then he heard the voice of the Devil saying: "PARIS, YOU HAVE SINNED . . ."

11

ATTITUDES AND INSULTS

Mackem Compliments:

'er, she could shoplift in a kebab shop.

At the conclusion of a more than satisfactory repast: "I've eaten worse."

You want to feel really handsome, svelte and successful? Go shopping at Tesco in Sunderland.

What's the difference between a Mackem and a sperm?

A sperm has one chance in ten million of becoming a human being.

How many Mackems does it take to change a light bulb?

It doesn't matter, they're all condemned to eternal darkness anyway.

What do you get when you cross a Mackem with a pig?

I don't know. There are some things a pig just won't do.

What's the difference between a wedding and a wake in Sunderland?

There's one less drunk at a wake.

Q. Why wasn't Jesus born in Sunderland?
A. Because God couldn't find three wise men and a virgin.

Why are they putting Mackems at the bottom of the sea?

They found out that deep down, they're really not so bad.

Two Mackems jump off a cliff, which one hits the ground first?

Who gives a fuck?

Mackems got into the gene pool when the lifeguard wasn't looking.

One-celled organisms out-score them in IQ tests.

Prime candidates for natural deselection.

Mackems are so dense that light bends around them.

If you stand close enough to a Mackem, you can hear the sea.

Dead Mackems: why aren't there more?

12

MENTAL WELLNESS

NHS cutbacks are going a bit far. This is, allegedly, the message you receive when you phone a particular hospital in Sunderland:

"Hello, you have reached the Psychiatric Clinic.

If you are obsessive-compulsive, press 1 repeatedly.

If you are co-dependent, have someone press 2 for you.

If you are paranoid, we know who you are. Stay on the line so we can trace this call.

If you suffer from multiple personality disorder, press 3, 4 and 5.

If you are suffering from a schizophrenic personality disorder, wait for a little voice to tell you which number to press.

If you are paranoid-delusional, we know who you are and what you want. Just stay on the line so we can trace the call.

If you are depressed, it doesn't matter which number you press. No one will answer. Ever.

If you are delusional and occasionally hallucinate,

please be aware that the thing you are holding to the side of your head is alive and about to bite your ear off."

The psychology instructor at the same Sunderland hospital had just finished a lecture on mental health and was giving an oral test.

Speaking specifically about manic depression, she asked: "How would you diagnose a patient who walks back and forth screaming at the top of his lungs one minute, then sits in a chair weeping uncontrollably the next?"

A Mackem at the back raised his hand and asked: "Newcastle's manager?"

13

ANOTHER WORD TO THE WISE

This is a real sign in a Sunderland shop:

"Warning to shoplifters: Anyone caught shoplifting will be gagged, beaten, whipped and tortured. Any survivors will be prosecuted to the full extent of the law."

Mackem Lord's Prayer

Our Lager,
Which art in barrels,
Hallowed be thy drink.
Thy will be drunk, (I will be drunk)
At home, as it is in the pub.
Give us this day our foamy head.
And forgive us our spillages,
As we forgive those who spill against us.
And lead us not to incarceration,
But deliver us from hangovers.
For thine is the beer, the heavy and the lager.
For ever and ever.
Barmen

A keen Mackem lad applied for a salesman's job. The supervisor asked him, "Have you ever been a salesman before?"

He replied confidently that he had. The guy liked the cut of his jib and said, "You can start tomorrow and I'll come and see you when we close up."

The day was long and arduous for the young man, but finally 5 o'clock came around. The supervisor duly turned up and asked: "How many sales did you make today?"

"One," said the Mackem.

"Only one?" he said. "Most of the staff make 20 or 30 sales a day. How much was the sale worth?"

"Three hundred thousand pounds," said the young man with a cheeky Mackem grin.

"How did you manage that?" asked the flabbergasted boss.

"Well," said the salesman, "this guy came in and I sold him a little fish hook, then a medium hook and finally a really big hook. Then I sold him a small fishing line, a medium one and a huge big one. I asked him where he was going fishing and he said down the coast.

I said he would probably need a boat, so I took him down to the boat department and sold him that twenty-footer with the twin engines. Then he said his Volkswagen probably wouldn't be able to pull it,

so I took him to the car department and sold him a great big 4-wheeler."

The supervisor took two steps back and asked in astonishment: "You sold all that to a guy who came in for a fish hook?"

"No," answered the Mackem. "He came in to buy a box of Tampax for his wife and I said to him: 'Your weekend's knackered, pal. You might as well go fishing.'"

14

TRUE STORY

A Mackem schoolteacher injured his back over the summer holidays and had to wear a plaster cast around the upper part of his body. It fitted neatly under his shirt and was not noticeable at all.

On the first day of his new school, still with the cast under his shirt, he found himself assigned to the worst behaved class in the school in one of Newcastle's worst estates.

He walked into the rowdy classroom, opened the window as wide as possible and then busied himself with desk work. When a strong breeze made his tie flap, he took the stapler from his desk and stapled the tie to his chest. Oddly, he had no trouble with discipline that year, and for the next few years he was known as The Iron Mackem.

15

ARSEHOLE, LOOPHOLE

What's the definition of a good Newcastle accountant?

Someone who has a loophole named after him.

16

A WUNCH OF BANKERS

A torn-arsed Mackem in trackies walks into a Newcastle bank and says to the female teller: "I want to open a fuckin' account." To which the woman replied: "I beg your pardon, what did you say?"

"Listen, I said I want to open a fuckin' account right now."

"I'm sorry sir, but we do not tolerate that kind of language in this bank," she replied.

Then the woman left her desk and went through to the bank manager and told him about her situation. They both returned and the manager asked: "What seems to be the problem here?"

"There's no bastard problem," the man said. "I just won 16 million quid in the lottery and I want to open a fuckin' account at this fuckin' bank!"

"I see, sir," the manager said. "And this fucking bitch is giving you grief?"

17

HOUSEY HOUSEY

Q: How do you get four old ladies in Hendon to swear?

A: Get the fifth old woman to shout: "Bingo!"

18

PLUS CA CHANGE

A returned Sunderland exile gets in a taxi at the airport and asks to be taken into town. He falls into conversation, as you do, with the taxi driver, and winds up claiming that even after twenty years away he can still recognise Sunderland districts by their smell and by how the air feels.

The driver takes up the challenge and produces a blindfold. (As they do, if asked.) They reach the first district and the guy opens the window, sticks his hand out, finger and thumb rubbing the air, takes a deep breath and says; "Thorney Close." He is of course right and the taxi driver asks: "How do you do that?" The guy says: "Oh, I can feel that edge of capitalist competition, that 'I must keep up with the Joneses', bigger car, better house. Not too pleasant. Bit like Newcastle."

The driver then takes him to another district and the guy goes through the same procedure, sticking his arm out etc and says: "East End," then explains: "I can feel all of the nationalities that came here seeking refuge from torture, imprisonment and

death in their former countries, their aspirations for their children, the hope that they will be accepted as new Mackems. I wish them well."

The driver is impressed and decides on one final test for the passenger. They get there and one second after he has stuck his hand out and before he has even taken a breath, he says: "Pennywell."

The driver says: "Jees, that was quick. How can you possibly know?"

The guy says: "My watch is gone."

Geordies who wish to convert this story to their native city have a wide choice of final district. You know where they are.

Sign on the roadside near a Sunderland hospital:
Hospital Quiet Zone.
Please Use Silencers On Your Shooters.

Sticker on a Sunderland car:
Toot if you love peace and quiet.

Another sticker on a chav car:
Pardon my driving, I am reloading.

19

MACKEMS DO GRASS

One afternoon a wealthy Geordie lawyer was driving home from a hard day robbing Mackems when he saw two men along the roadside eating grass. Curious, he stopped and got out to investigate.

"Why are you eating grass?" he asked one man.

"We don't have any money for food," said the guy, "so we have to eat grass."

"Well then, you can come with me to my house and I'll feed you," the Geordie said.

"But I have a wife and two children. They're over there underneath that tree," said the guy pathetically.

"That's fine," replies the lawyer. "Bring them along too."

Turning to the other poor soul he stated: "You can come with us too."

The second man, in a pitiful voice, said, "But I have a wife and SIX children with me, some of them mine."

"Don't worry about it," the lawyer replies casually. "You can bring them along as well."

They all entered the car, which was no easy task, as even the vast 4×4 nearly wasn't quite big enough.

Once underway, one of the poor guys turned to the lawyer and said, "You are very kind, new friend. Thank you for taking all of us with you."

The Geordie replied. "Glad to do it. You'll love my place. The grass is nearly a foot high!"

Another couple from the terraces.

Build a bonfire,
Build a bonfire,
Put the Mackems on the top,
Put the city in the middle,
And then burn the fucking lot.

Feed the Mackems,
Let them know it's Christmas time,
Feed the Mackems,
Let them know it's Christmas time,
etc.

20

A MORAL

The Mackem teacher gave her class an exercise: Get their parents to tell them a story with a moral.

The next day the kids came back and one by one began to tell their stories.

"Johnny, do you have a story to share?"

"Yes, miss, my daddy told me a story about my Auntie Mel. Auntie Mel was a pilot in Iraq and her plane was hit. She had to bail out over enemy territory and all she had was two bottles of Buckfast, a gun and a survival knife. She drank the Buckfast on the way down so it would not break and then her parachute landed her right in the middle of twenty enemy troops. She shot fifteen of them with the gun until she ran out of bullets and killed four more with the knife till the blade broke and then she killed the last Iraqi with her bare hands and her teeth, biting his throat out."

"Jesus!" said the horrified teacher. "What kind of moral did your daddy tell you from that horrible story?"

Johnny replied: "Stay well away from Auntie Mel when she's been drinking."

21

THE LORD GOD AND GEORDIES

Standing on the seashore, a Geordie lady on her holidays watches her grandson playing with the rubbish in the water. She is thunderstruck when she sees a huge wave crash over him. When it recedes, the boy is no longer there. He has vanished.

Screaming, the woman holds her hands to the sky and cries, "Lord, how could you? Have I not been a wonderful mother and grandmother? Have I not scrimped and saved so I could give to the church? Have I not always put others before myself? Have I not always turned my other cheek and loved my neighbours? Have I not –"

A deep, loud Mackem voice from the sky interrupts. "Moan, moan, moan, moan. Gizza break, here!"

Immediately, another huge wave appears and crashes on the beach. And when it recedes, the boy is there smiling, splashing around as if nothing ever happened.

The deep loud voice continues. "There's your lad back. Are you happy now?"

The Geordie lady responded: "He had a hat."

22

ERUDITE INSULTS

If you live in Sunderland, then being awake is not necessarily a desirable state.

In Sunderland, you're considered posh if you have slates on your roof. Indeed, if you have a roof.

If you take a picture of a Mackem, he runs about claiming you've stolen his soul.

23

DRY HUMOUR

Two Mackems are walking down the road in Newcastle when they see a sign in a shop window. Suits £15, shirts £2, trousers £2.50. One said to the other one: "Look at that – we could buy a lot of that gear and, when we get back to Sunderland we could make a fortune. When we go into the shop don't say anything, let me do all the talking, cause if they hear our right accent they might not serve us, so I'll speak in my best Newcastle voice."

They go in and he orders, in his best attempt at a Geordie voice, 50 suits at £15, 100 shirts at £2 and 50 trousers at £2.50. The owner of the shop says: "You two are Mackems, aren't you?"

The Mackem replies: "Aye ok, lad, how the hell did you know that?"

The owner says: "This is a dry cleaners."

24

LITTLE DARLINGS

Little Mackem Billy walked into the house shortly before noon.

"Billy!" his mother cried. "What are you doing home from school so early?"

"I got the right answer to the question."

Beaming, his mother asked: "Which question was that?"

"Who put the dog shite on the teacher's chair. It was me."

25

STILL GAME

The prosecution and defence had both presented their final arguments in a case involving a Mackem accused of operating an illegal still. The judge turned to the jury and asked: "Before giving you your instructions, do any of you have any questions?"

"Yes, M'lud," replied one of the jurors, a fellow estate dweller. "Did the defendant boil the malt one or two hours, how does he cool it quickly, and at what point does he add the yeast?"

26

DUMB MACKEMS

Geordie: "Did you ever hear that joke about the museum in Newcastle that had a skull of Queen Elizabeth the First when she was twelve in one room, and a skull when she was thirty in another?"

"No," said the Mackem. "What was it?"

Jimmy and Jack went into The New Monkey in great good humour and ordered two large whiskies.
"Are you lads celebrating something?" asked the barman.

"We are," said Jimmy. "We've just finished a jigsaw puzzle in record time. A hundred pieces it had, and it only took us six months."

"Six months? But that's quite a long time," said the barman.

"I don't think so," said Jack. "It said on the box, three to five years."

27

GOLF

"Sandy, you promised to be home at two o'clock this afternoon and now it's after six."

"Bonny wife, please. That Mackem I drew in the Medal is dead – dropped dead on the 4th green this morning."

"Oh, how terrible."

"It certainly was. The whole day, it's been: hit the ball . . . drag the Mackem . . . hit the ball . . . drag the Mackem."

28

NEWCASTLE'S FINEST

One of Newcastle's finest pulls over a Mackem who's been weaving in and out of the lanes. He goes up to the man's window and says: "Sir, I need you to blow into this breathalyser tube."

The man says, "Sorry, orifice, I can't do that. I am an asthmatic. If I do that, I'll have a really bad asthma attack."

"Okay, fine. I need you to come down to the station to give a blood sample."

"I can't do that either. I am a haemophiliac. If I do that, I'll bleed to death."

"Well, then, we need a urine sample."

"I'm sorry, officer, I can't do that either. I am also a diabetic. If I do that, I'll get really low blood sugar."

"All right, then I need you to come out here and walk this white line."

"I can't do that either, orifice."

"Why not?"

"Because I'm absolutely fuckin' drunk."

A Mackem lay sprawled across three entire stall seats in the Theatre Royal. When the usher came by and noticed this, he whispered to the man: "Sorry, sir, but you're only allowed one seat."

The man heard and looked up, but didn't budge.

The usher became impatient. "Sir, if you don't get up from there I'm going to have to call the manager."

This time the man made a gutteral sound, a very Mackem noise, which infuriated the usher, who turned and marched briskly back up the aisle in search of his manager. In a few moments, both the usher and the manager returned and stood over the man. Together the two of them tried repeatedly to move him, but with no success.

Finally, they summoned the police.

The large sub-unit of Newcastle's finest surveyed the situation briefly then asked: "All right, my friend, what's your name?"

"Jimmy," the man muttered.

"Oho," said the cop, having detected the Mackem accent. "Where are you from, Jimmy?"

With pain in his voice Jimmy replied: "The balcony."

Late one Friday night the policeman spotted a Sunderland man driving very erratically through the

streets of Newcastle. They pulled the man over and asked him if he had been drinking that evening.

"Yes, I have. It's Friday, you know, and I'm in a foreign city, so I stopped by a pub where I had six or seven pints. And then there was something called 'Happy Hour' and they served these huge voddies for pennies. I had four or five of them. Then I stopped on the way home to get another bottle for later. I've drunk some already." And the man fumbled around in his jacket until he located his bottle of vodka, which he held up for inspection.

The officer sighed, and said, "Sir, I'm afraid I'll need you to step out of the car and take a breathalyser test."

The Mackem said indignantly: "Why? Don't you believe me?"

29

RANT

Here's a young man who knows his own mind. He prefers to remain anonymous. There, there, let's go for a little lie down.

"Sunderland is a city that likes to boast about how culturally important it is, despite the fact that the only things to come out of Sunderland are criminals and fucking Kate Adie. It seems to be a Mackem law that whenever you go outside Sunderland, you must always tell everyone who looks at you that it is the funniest place on earth, full of the nicest people. I suspect this is a ploy to get more unsuspecting visitors for mugging. In reality, Sunderland is an absolute shithole, a city that seems to be held together using only graffiti, vomit and stacks of torn rubbish bags with the occasional used nappy that has been run over in the middle of the road. NOTHING funny EVER came out of Sunderland.

And don't get me started on the accent. Mackems do not speak English. They actually speak some strange Klingon dialect from a place where everyone

has chronic bronchitis. Sunderland truly is the sphincter of this planet, and any colonic irrigation should be sent their way as soon as possible. I fucking hate Sunderland and I hope that this little rant has somehow helped me to overcome the years of torture I had to go through constantly going there with my family. I hate it, I hate it, I fucking bloody well shagging HATE IT!"

And another nice one from the terraces:

In your Sunderland slums,
You look in the dustbin for something to eat,
You find a dead rat and you think it's a treat,
In your Sunderland slums.

In your Sunderland slums,
You shit on the carpet, you piss in the bath,
You finger your grandma, and think it's a laugh,
In your Sunderland slums.

In your Sunderland slums,
You speak in an accent that's thankfully rare,
You wear a pink tracksuit and have curly hair,
In your Sunderland slums.

In your Sunderland slums,
Your mum's on the game and your dad's in the nick,
You can't get a job 'cos you're too fucking thick,
In your Sunderland slums.

30

DRAFT MODERN MATHEMATICS PAPER 2008

HIGHLY CONFIDENTIAL
SUNDERLAND REGION

Name. . . . .
Nickname. . . . .
Gangname. . . . .

Steven the Stabber has bought half a kilo of cocaine for large. He wants to make 300% on the deal and still pay Mad Malcolm his 10% protection money. How much must he charge for a gram?

Tiny David reckons he'll get £42.50 extra Marriage Allowance a week if he ties the knot with Fat Alice. Even if he steals the ring, the wedding will cost him £587. And he'll have to start buying two portions of fish and chips every night instead of one. How long will it be before David wishes he'd stayed single?

Joey and Billy stole a 1999 green Toyota 1600GL with 35,000 on the clock – and got a grand for it. How much more would they have got if it had been metallic silver, done 29,000 miles and had low profile tyres?

Jake the Flake and Fingers got grassed up for dealing speed. The Flake got 18 months but Fingers got 3 years. How many more previous convictions did Fingers have?

EXTRA CREDIT: Who was Fingers' brief?

31

TO BE SURE, TO BE SURE

Three men are sitting in the maternity ward of a hospital waiting for the imminent birth of their respective children. One is a Geordie, one a Mackem and the other a West Indian. They are all very nervous and pacing the floor – as you do in these situations.

Suddenly the doctor bursts through the double doors saying: "Gentlemen you won't believe this but your wives have all had their babies within five minutes of each other."

The men are beside themselves with happiness and joy. "And," said the doctor, "They have all had little boys." The fathers are ecstatic and congratulate each other over and over. "However, we do have one slight problem," the doctor said. "In all the confusion we may have mixed the babies up getting them to the nursery and would be grateful if you could join us there to try and help identify them."

With that the Geordie raced past the doctor and bolted to the nursery. Once inside he picked up a

dark skinned infant with dreadlocks saying: "There's no doubt about it, this boy is mine!"

The doctor looked bewildered and said: "Well sir, of all the babies I would have thought that maybe this child could be of West Indian descent."

"That's a maybe," said the Geordie, "but one of the other two is a Mackem and I'm not taking the risk!"

32

FOOTBALL

The Post Office has just recalled their latest stamps. They had pictures of Sunderland players on them and people couldn't work out which side to spit on.

And some Toon tunes:

Toon, Toon,
Hate the Mackems,
Toon, Toon,
Hate the Mackems.

When I was a little bitty boy,
My grandmother bought me a cute little toy,
Two Sunderland fans, hanging on a string,
She told me to kick their fucking heads in.
Mackems on a string,
Mackems on a string,
She told me to kick their fucking heads in.
Mackems on a string,
Mackems on a string,
She told me to kick their fucking heads in.

Toon-Toon-Toon!   Everybody   say   Whey-Aye!
 Whey-Aaaaaaye!
Toon-Toon-Toon!   Everybody   say   Whey-Aye!
 Whey-Aaaaaaye!

Bye Bye Sunderland
You're not coming back
Read my lips you are fucking crap

33

YOU KNOW THAT YOU ARE LIVING IN A SUNDERLAND ESTATE WHEN:

Your standard of living improves when you go camping.

Your neighbour has asked to borrow half a can of beer.

None of the tyres on your van are the same size.

You can get heroin delivered.

Your bin man is confused about what goes and what stays.

You actually wear shoes your dog brought home.

You've been in a punch-up at a jumble sale.

You carry a baseball bat in the front seat of your van so you can pacify the kids in the back.

34

CHAVS

Chavs are the genital warts on the scrotum of society.
The Sunderland Chav can be recognised in a number of ways:

1) The males will most certainly be wearing some form of tracksuit, probably Lacoste, with a not-so-matching pair of Rockport boots. The females, the Chavettes, usually delight in sporting the latest in sunbed fashion ("A pound for forty five minutes? I'll 'ave a go"), along with something revealing, such as a social security form tucked into their miniskirt.

2) A bloke with his hand down his crotch is a dead giveaway, as is a cap in any shape or form.

3) The females often sport a post-coital bump, usually uncovered, with a fag in one hand and their favourite bottle of peroxide in the other. How else do you explain year round bleach blonde hair, with no sign of roots?

4) Chavlings (the spawn of adult Chavs) are

usually recognised on the streets between 9am and 3pm weekdays, often riding a bicycle, which has usually been stolen. Their sole purpose is to follow in the footsteps of their mothers. The father is not usually known.

A good way to spot a chavette is that they wear earrings you could drive a bus through.

Legalised Chav Hunting

We can advertise and promote to all would-be big game hunters. At £10,000 a bullet the Government could use the cash to subsidise the cost of the average Chav/chavette seven child family, until through natural selection they themselves become the endangered species. Survival of the fittest would never become more relevant. How many Buckfast and cheap cider drinkers can outrun an open top Jeep with four overweight Americans equipped with sniper rifles and a highly-paid local guide?

Rules:
1. Anything in Kappa, Burberry etc is fair game.
2. See Rule 1

Benefits:

Within two to four years large sections of Sunderland would be open to all once more. JJB

Sports, Sports Division etc, would all close and Income and Council Tax will reduce.

Or possibly:

Far from being a blight on our communities a chav can both brighten our cities and educate our children, provided of course we have suitable containment. We would be able to surround them with high voltage enclosures such as those being used in our more modern jails. Visitors to the attraction would be able to see wild herds of the Common Chav hanging around at the base of authentically re-built housing blocks or trying to make rollies whilst swigging MD 20/20 at bus stops. Tours would be conducted in the shells of burnt-out police cars so as not to attract the attentions of the chavs. If, however, a tourist were approached by any of the chavs, the burnt-out police cars would be equipped with sound recordings of a school. This being the most alien of all sounds to a chav, he would be temporally confused and need a fix of spray solvent to help clear his mind.

There would be gift shops with shuttered windows and screens in front of the counters to enable young Cheeky Chavs to mingle with tourists and staff. Staff would be Working Chavs and heavily pregnant Chavettes, all trained to serve with an air

of contempt for being made to do anything. Tourists and staff would have toilet facilities provided on every vertical concrete surface and any secluded passageways between shops or buildings. Attached to the safari part of the attraction would be a fun park offering a full range of chav pastimes. The choices of activities would include: Driving around slowly listening to anything sub 20 hertz, allowing the squeaky whine of your Cruiser Chav guide to be heard above the pounding bass, and driving around quickly as above, but trying to throw all contraband out the window before the police catch up with you. If you were to favour more intellectual pursuits there would be daily games of Who Wants To Be a Millionaire: The Benefits Edition and The Weakest Genetic Link.

All patrons would receive lasting memories of their trip in the form of either a facial stab wound, severe tooth and gum disease, acute cholesterol problems or a photograph taken at the moment their first hit off the crack-pipe took effect.

And some chavlines

Q. What is the difference between a dying Chav and an onion?
A. Onions make you cry.

Q. Why are Chavs like slinkies?
A. They have no real use but it's great to watch one fall down a flight of stairs.

Q. What do you call a Chavette in a white track-suit?
A. The bride.

Q. What's the difference between a Chav and a coconut?
A. One's thick and hairy, the other's a coconut.

Q. How do you get 100 Chavs into a phone box?
A. Paint three stripes on it.

Q. Two Chavs in a car without any music. Who's driving?
A. The police.

And of course there are the Mackemcharvers, aka chavs, but specifically from Sunderland.

Is that a dog turd over there or a Mackem taking a rest?

Mackems are a government experiment which involved breeding rats and humans and has gone

terribly wrong. Originally intended to create a type of drone army but instead created an ever-increasing group of city-dwelling smegma piles that live in tower blocks or boxes. It has recently been discovered that these genetically modified rats have little or no intelligence and only survive on basic instinct. Instead of fighting wars these vermin fight random people for "looking at them," will only fight one normal person at a time and there has to be at least 50 Mackems before any combat takes place. They also steal from old people, off licences and cars. Doesn't matter what it is, it could be a comb they'll still have it.

General Mackemcharver Image
Mackems are often easy to spot as they hang around together and all look the same, whiteish (sometimes green), greasy, spotty short haired, covered in "gold" jewellery (crafted by the finest £1 shop usually made from copper, tin, plastic etc). And of course the trackie bottoms, white sports socks, a woolly jumper/hooded over-throw jacket, baseball cap that teeters on the back of the head, white mucky trainers/fuck off pair of boots. They are unable to speak coherently.

Still, Mackems do maintain some sort of social/military structure. Be aware of the following invading your town:

Foot Mackem

Aged 13–16, they hang round outside off-licences, corners, parks. Uniformed in the mandatory Adidas trackie bottoms tucked into white kappa sports socks. Any type of classic trainer: Adidas/Reebok (Rockport boots worn for nights out). Weapons of choice: tin of spray paint, glass bottle.

Commander Mackem

Aged 17–20, requires a vehicle of some sort, usually a Vauxhall Nova, Astra, Ford Escort, Sierra, Suzuki 125 Trailblazer (used generally for snatching old ladies' handbags), all of which have been modified using scrap metal, Polyfilla, drainpipes and Lego. Dress code still the same as taste is not a quality found in any Mackem. Weapon of choice, a baseball bat or a plank of wood located in the driver's side footwell, and "gold" knuckledusters.

General Mackem

There only can ever be one General Mackem to each group of about 30 Mackems (6 Commanders, 18 Foot, 6 female Mackemettes). A Mackem leader is primitive looking, has to be over 25-years-old, have a criminal record which include any of these: burglary, theft, ABH, GBH and generally being offensive. Has to own a pair of jeans and a shirt, requires some sort of facial hair, have what may be classed as a human girlfriend, to be a father, and to have his own

bedsit and sell drugs. In some cases addicted to heroin. Uniformed in a classic full all-white Adidas tracksuit, Rockport boots nicely trimmed with the finest gold jewellery from Argos.

Weapon of choice: an air rifle, a piece of scaffolding, Alsatian or Rottweiler dog.

What do you call a Mackem in a box?
Innit.

What do you call a Mackem in a filing cabinet?
Sorted.

What do you call a Mackem on a bike?
A thief.

What do you call a Mackem in a car?
Arrested.

What do you call a Mackem in a bank?
A thief.

What do you call a Mackem in a fridge?
Chillin'.

What do you call a Mackem in a bus shelter?
At a party.

What do you call a 12-year-old Mackem girl?
Pregnant.

What do you call a Mackem girl without child?
Under the age of 10.

Why did the Mackem cross the road?
To punch someone for no reason.

What's a Mackem's favourite car?
One without an alarm.

What do you call a Mackem in a coffin?
A damn good reason to kill another.

What do you call two dead Mackems?
A good start to the day.

What do Mackems use as protection during sex?
A bus shelter.

What do you say to a Mackem with a job?
Can I have a Big Mac please?

What's the difference between a dead fox and a dead
    Mackem in the road?
The dead fox has skid marks in front of it.

What do you call a 30-year-old Mackemette ?
Dunno, ask her 17-year-old son.

What do you do if you run a Mackem over?
Slip it into reverse just to make sure.

35

SUNDERLAND BANTER

Grow your own dope. Plant a Mackem.

Q. What's the first question at a Sunderland pub quiz?
A. What are you looking at?

Q. Why does the River Wear run through Sunderland?
A. Because if it walked it would be mugged.

Q. What do you call a Mackem in a three-bed-room semi?
A. A burglar.

To a theatre audience:

"Have you all switched off your mobile phones? And have the people from Sunderland turned off their electronic tags?"

Mackems consider themselves well dressed if their socks match.

36

HOW TO HANDLE STRESS

Picture yourself near a stream.

Birds are softly chirping in the crisp, cool mountain air.

Nothing can bother you here. No one knows this secret place.

You are in total seclusion from that place called "the world".

The soothing sound of a gentle waterfall fills the air with a cascade of serenity.

The water is clear. You can easily make out the face of the person whose head you're holding under the water.

There now . . . feeling better?

A Mackem goes to his doctor to find out what's wrong with him.

"Your problem is that you are fat," says the doctor.

"I'd like a second opinion," responds the man.

"Okay," replies the doctor, "you are ugly too."

HORSE'S ASK

The aspiring psychiatrists were attending their first class on emotional extremes. "Just to establish some parameters," said the professor to the student from Ryhope, "what is the opposite of joy?"

"Sadness," said the student.

"And the opposite of depression?" he asked of the young lady from Plains Farm.

"Elation," said she.

"And you," he said to the young man from the East End, "how about the opposite of woe?"

The Mackem replied, "I think that that would be giddy-up."

38

OOOH CONTROVERSIAL

Description of the election process in Newcastle: "Poli," in Latin meaning "many" and "tics" meaning "blood-sucking creatures".

Warning
"He needed killin'," is a valid defence in Sunderland courts.

The top 10 things not to say to a Mackem cop when you get stopped for speeding:

I can't reach my licence unless you hold my Buckfast.

Sorry officer, I didn't realize my radar detector wasn't plugged in.

You must have been doing 125 to keep up with me, excellent driving.

I thought you had to be in relatively good physical shape to be a police officer.

You're not going to check the boot, are you?

I pay your wages, lad.

Great officer, that's terrific. The last monkey only gave me a warning as well.

I was trying to keep up with traffic. Yes, I know there are no other cars about, that's how far they are ahead of me.

Well, when I reached down to pick up my bag of crack, my shotgun fell off my lap and got stuck between the brake and the accelerator, forcing me to speed.

What do you mean 'have I been drinking?' You're the trained specialist.

39

SCHOOL TALES, TALL AND TRUE

Somewhere in darkest Sunderland, an Attendance Officer accompanied by a Deputy Head (safety in numbers) went into a block of flats to speak to a family about the daughter's poor attendance.

As they climbed the stairs they spotted a large Rottweiler patrolling the landing outside the flat they were going to visit. Undaunted by this slavering beast, they rang the bell. The door was opened and in rushed the dog. They were greeted by the mother and taken into the barely furnished living room.

The conversation wasn't going too well and to make matters worse, the Deputy Head saw the dog cock its leg and pee up against a wall in the room. Nobody said anything and he decided to keep quiet.

The conversation became more heated and then he saw the dog do a shit in the corner. Again nobody mentioned it.

Eventually the Attendance Officer decided to call a halt to the meeting as the family were becomingly increasingly hostile towards their callers.

They were shown out somewhat abruptly and started to walk downstairs, both glad to have escaped, when the flat door was thrown open and the father shouted after them:

"An' you can take your fucking dog with you!"

One day a boy went into his Classics class and placed a lump of rock on his teacher's desk. When the teacher asked where this rock had come from, the pupil replied: "It's a present from my big brother (a former pupil). He was in Greece with the army and he chipped a bit off the Parthenon for you!"

These immortal words were heard during a typical heated class discussion:

"Aye, and you've got a face like a second hand dart-board!"

In a recent written Home Economics test in Sunderland on cookery, the pupils were asked to write down the names of three typical Mackem dishes.

One pupil carefully wrote: "A plate, a cup and a saucer."

40

DOGGED SUPER SALESMAN

When the shop manager of a large Newcastle tailor's returned from lunch, he noticed that the sales assistant's hand was bandaged, but before he could ask about the bandage the guy said he had some very good news for him.

"Guess what?" he said. "I finally sold that terrible suit we've had on the rack for so long."

"Do you mean that repulsive pink-and-orange double-breasted monstrosity?" the manager asked.

"The very one."

"That's brilliant," the manager cried, "I thought we'd never get rid of that horrible thing. That had to be the ugliest suit we've ever had. But why is your hand bandaged?"

The salesman replied: "It was David Blunkett that bought it, and his guide dog bit me."

41

ANOTHER GOOD DOG

Four men were boasting about how clever their dogs were. The first man was an engineer, the second man was an accountant, the third man was a chemist and the fourth was from Hendon.

To show off, the engineer said to his dog: "Protractor, do your trick." Protractor trotted over to a desk, took out some paper and a pen, and promptly drew a circle, a square, and a triangle.

Everyone agreed that was pretty clever. However, the accountant said his dog could do better. He called his dog and said: "Slide Rule, do your trick." Slide Rule went into the kitchen, returned with a dozen biscuits and divided them into four equal piles of three each.

Everyone agreed that was pretty good, but the chemist said his dog could do better. He called his dog and said: "Measure, do your trick." Measure got up, walked to the fridge in the kitchen, took out a pint of milk, got a glass from the cupboard and poured exactly a half pint without spilling a drop.

Everyone agreed that was good. The three men turned to the Mackem and said, "What can your dog do?" He called to his dog and said: "Catkiller, do your trick." Catkiller jumped to his feet, ate the biscuits, drank the milk, peed on the paper, sexually assaulted the other three dogs, claimed he injured his back while doing so, filed a complaint about unsafe working conditions, put in for compen and went home on the Pat and Mick.

42

AND FINALLY, A LAST CALL

It was Mackem Pat's last day on the job after 35 years of carrying the post through all kinds of weather to the same neighbourhoods of Newcastle. Everybody knew Mackem Pat, though they didn't of course speak to him much.

But surprise! When he arrived at the first house, he was greeted by the whole family there, who all hugged and congratulated him and sent him on his way with a cheque for £50.

At the second house they presented him with superb Cuban cigars in an 18-carat gold box, while the folk at the third house gave him a case of 30-year-old Scotch.

At the fourth house he was met at the door by a stunning blonde in her lingerie. She took him by the arm and led him up the stairs to the bedroom where she blew his mind with the most passionate love he had ever experienced.

When he had had enough they went downstairs, where the woman made him a giant breakfast: eggs, tomatoes, bacon, sausage, beans, black pudding, the

complete heart-stopper, and freshly-squeezed orange juice. When he was truly satisfied she poured him a cup of steaming coffee.

As she was pouring, he noticed a five pound note sticking out from under the cup's bottom edge. "All this was just too wonderful for words," he said, "but what's the fiver for?"

"Well," said the blonde, "last night, I told my husband that today would be your last day, and that we should do something special for you. I asked him what to give you. He said: 'Fuck him. Give him a fiver.' The breakfast was my idea."